AF581190

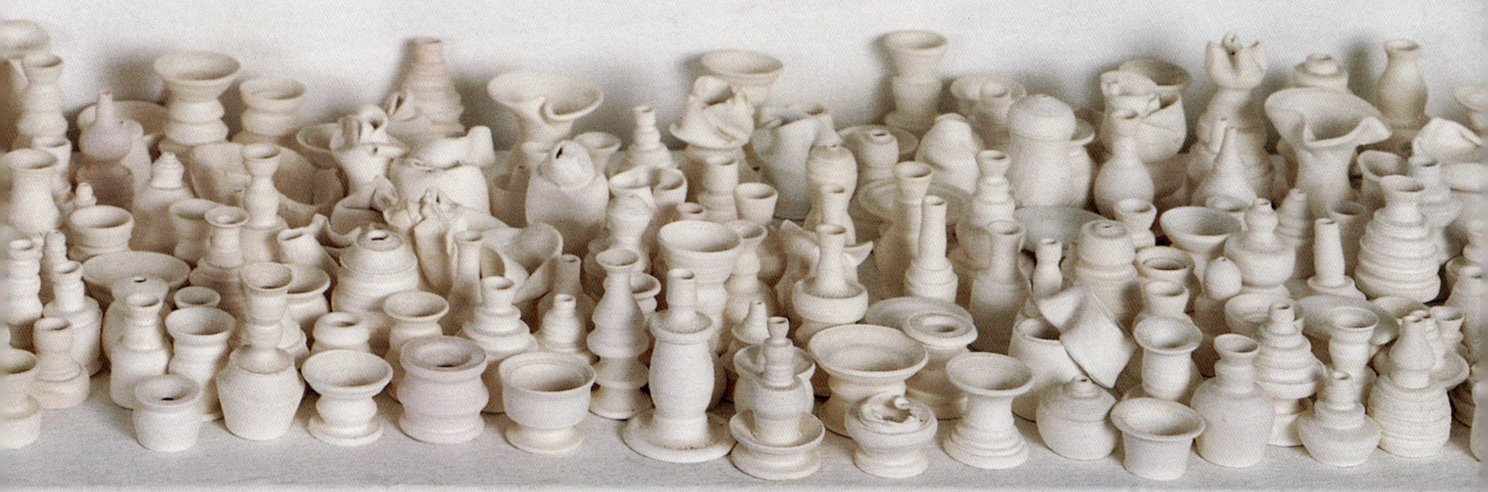

Charles LeDray, Sculpture 1989-2002

Curator, Claudia Gould

Institute of Contemporary Art
University of Pennsylvania, Philadelphia

May 11–July 14, 2002

EXHIBITION TOUR SCHEDULE

Institute of Contemporary Art
University of Pennsylvania
Philadelphia, Pennsylvania
May 11 – July 14, 2002

The Arts Club of Chicago
Chicago, Illinois
September 20 – December 21, 2002

Yerba Buena Center for the Arts
San Francisco, California
January 25 – April 6, 2003

Seattle Art Museum
Seattle, Washington
April 26 – July 27, 2003

Lenders to the Exhibition

Ralph Balass
Ruth and Jake Bloom
Frank Cohen
Kenneth L. Freed
Carol and Arthur Goldberg
Susan and Michael Hort
Barbara and Leonard Kaban
Eileen and Peter Norton
Nancy and Joel Portnoy
San Francisco Museum
of Modern Art
Robert J. Shiffler
Sperone Westwater
Walter Sudol and
Steven Johnson
Whitney Museum
of American Art
Merrill Wright
Private Collection
Private Collection, London
Private Collection, New York
Private Collection, New York
Private Collection, New York

Institute of Contemporary Art, University of Pennsylvania, Philadelphia May 11 – July 14, 2002

"Charles LeDray, Sculpture 1989-2002" exhibition and catalog are funded by The Andy Warhol Foundation for the Visual Arts and the members of ICA's New York Leadership Circle: Christopher J. Carrera Foundation, Jason and Ashley Bernhard, James Berman and Lisa Rechsteiner, Debra and Craig S. Cogut, Christopher and Cecile D'Amelio, The Ellen and Gary S. Davis Foundation, David and Virginia Ford / The Ford Family Foundation, Glenn R. Fuhrman, Lori T. Moore, Lauren and Gerardo Rosenkranz, Allison and Neil Rubler, Geoffrey and Melissa Greener, K. Hovnanian Enterprises, Inc., Anurag Bhargava, Alice J. Blank and David S. Udell, Robert Fogelson, James Gray, Eric S. Lane, Maria Parker Paumgarten and John Parker, John C. Phelan and Amy Merriman, Kevin Raidy, Pamela and Arthur Sanders, Daniel C. Scheffey, Joey and Christopher Schlank, and Maggie and Amor Towles. Additional support has been provided by The Horace W. Goldsmith Foundation, Commonwealth of Pennsylvania Council on the Arts, The Dietrich Foundation Inc., the Overseers Board for the Institute of Contemporary Art, friends and members of ICA, and the University of Pennsylvania. (Information complete as of 1/24/02.)

 University of Pennsylvania 118 South 36th Street. Philadelphia, PA 19104-3289. ISBN 0-88454-099-5. Library of Congress Catalog Card No. 2002101066. Design: Twelvetrees Publishers, Santa Fe, New Mexico. Printed and bound in Korea. Editing: Gerald Zeigerman, Philadelphia. Photography Credits: Jean Brasilla / Villa Arson, D. James Dee, John Groo, Guy L'Heureux, Tom Powel, Oren Slor, Beth Wessen.

Contents

Come Together, 1995–96
Fabric, thread,
embroidery floss, metal
34 ½ x 26 x 6 ¼ inches
Collection San Francisco
Museum of Modern Art,
San Francisco
Purchased through a gift
of Kimberly S. L. Knight
and John B. Knight III

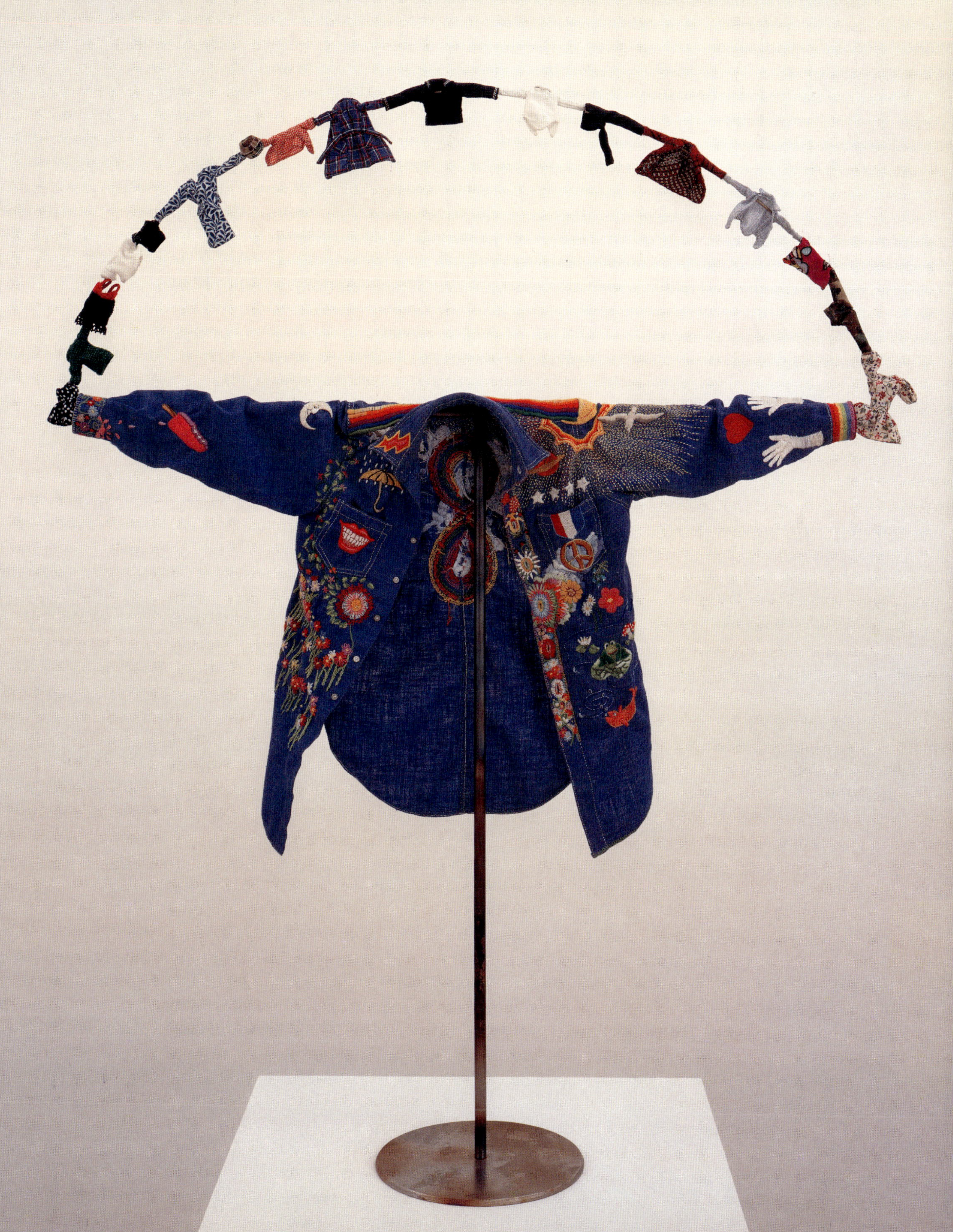

Acknowledgments **Claudia Gould, Director**

It is with pride that ICA presents "Charles LeDray, Sculpture 1989–2002," the first museum survey of this artist's work. We are grateful to the individuals and organizations that have generously agreed to lend work, as well as the funders who have helped make the exhibition possible.

Nearly ten years ago, at the Tom Cugliani Gallery in New York, I saw my first Charles LeDray exhibition. Three years later, at Jay Gorney Modern Art, I saw the second one-person show of his work. Jay Gorney, now of Gorney, Bravin, and Lee, was instrumental in having me take a longer look at Charles when I arrived at ICA. I thank both Tom and Jay for this enduring experience. It is, however, with the Sperone Westwater Gallery that I have spent my time working over the past year. The director, David Leiber, has become a confidant; his genteel manner, tenacity, and humor have kept me on track. In addition, Angela Westwater has been very helpful in providing guidance to us all. From their staff, Karen Polack has proven a key resource for curatorial details. Sperone Weswater's support for this show is indicative of its ardent commitment to the work of Charles LeDray.

I want to thank the lenders to this exhibition, many of whom have been lending their work to ICA for a number of years. Because we are a noncollecting institution, their generosity is essential to our success.

The exhibition and catalog have been made possible by a considerable grant from The Andy Warhol Foundation for the Visual Arts: At The Warhol Foundation, I thank Pamela Clapp and Yona Backer for their guidance. ICA's New York Leadership Circle has also supported the exhibition. This group of Penn alumni was formed by Christopher D'Amelio (C88), who planted the initial idea in our heads, with the help of Glenn Fuhrman (W87, WG88), Neil Rubler (W98), and Pam Sanders (C78). The New York Leadership Circle now has many members and is raising money to fund a show each year at ICA; Charles LeDray is the first. Christopher J. Carrera (C88) challenged members of the New York Leadership Circle, and matched what they had raised one-to-one. I am particularly grateful for this group's dedication to and love of the ICA and contemporary art. I am indebted to those providing additional support—The Horace W. Goldsmith Foundation, Commonwealth of Pennsylvania Council on the Arts, The Dietrich Foundation Inc., the Board of Overseers for the Institute of Contemporary Art, our friends and members, and the University of Pennsylvania.

This show will be traveling to three venues after it leaves the ICA. I wish to thank Kathy Cottong, director, and Annette Ferrara, assistant to the diector, at The Arts Club of Chicago; John R. Killacky, executive director, Renny Pritikin, chief curator, and Rene de Guzman, visual arts coordinator at the Yerba Buena Center for the Arts, in San Francisco; and Mimi Gardner Gates, director, Lisa Corrin, deputy director of art, and Tara Young, assistant curator of modern and contemporary art, at the Seattle Art Museum for joining us in this presentation.

The ICA staff was essential in organizing this exhibition. Ingrid Schaffner, senior curator, is my sounding board, and I always appreciate her insight. Registrar and exhibitions coordinator, Robert Chaney, extended himself well beyond his normal duties, assisting in the traveling exhibition as well as helping secure the loans and making the shipping arrangements. Lindsay Lansdale, publications coordinator, has organized this catalog, and has helped us meet deadlines unheard of in the world of museum publications. Elyse Gonzales, assistant curator, and Bennett Simpson, Whitney-Lauder Curatorial Fellow, have helped me edit and organize the interview with the artist. Betsy Meyer, education coordinator, has worked to refine programs relevant to this exhibition for adults and children; I thank her for her dedication to ICA over the years. Preparator Clint Takeda and his installation crew have been a dream to work with, given the delicate nature of LeDray's sculptures. Our development office, under the direction of Marilyn H. Pollick and her team, Carolyne Chandler-Krull, and Joseph D. Kelly II, has been invaluable in securing the funds for well over eighteen months to make this exhibition happen. John McInerney, marketing and public relations coordinator, has been instrumental in our press initiatives. Cassandra Green, business administrator, has managed all the financial and logistical aspects of the exhibition, and my assistant, Carlene Ryan, has kept me sane. In addition, we all wish to thank Jim Smith, our front desk attendant, for his dedication and spirit. I must also thank the many volunteers who assist ICA throughout the course of a season.

Russell Ferguson has written a solid essay on the work of Charles LeDray; I thank him for agreeing to work with us on this publication. Gerald Zeigerman, our editor, has skillfully amended and polished the text. Jack Woody, of Twelvetrees Publishers, in Santa Fe, has created a beautiful catalog. His energy and humor here made our task much easier. I wish to thank Arlyn Eve Nathan for her patience and persistence with the design of the catalog.

Katherine Sachs, our chairperson, and the entire Board of Overseers at ICA have helped us realize an amazing season, which concludes with this exhibition. Their unconditional support of all our activities must be acknowledged.

Last, I wish to thank Charles LeDray for his years of fine work. It is our privilege to present his first museum exhibition.

FOLLOWING PAGE:
S.A.M., 1994
Fabric, thread, metal, plastic, paint
25 ¼ x 11 x 4 inches
Courtesy of Merrill Wright, Seattle, Washington
Photo: Oren Slor

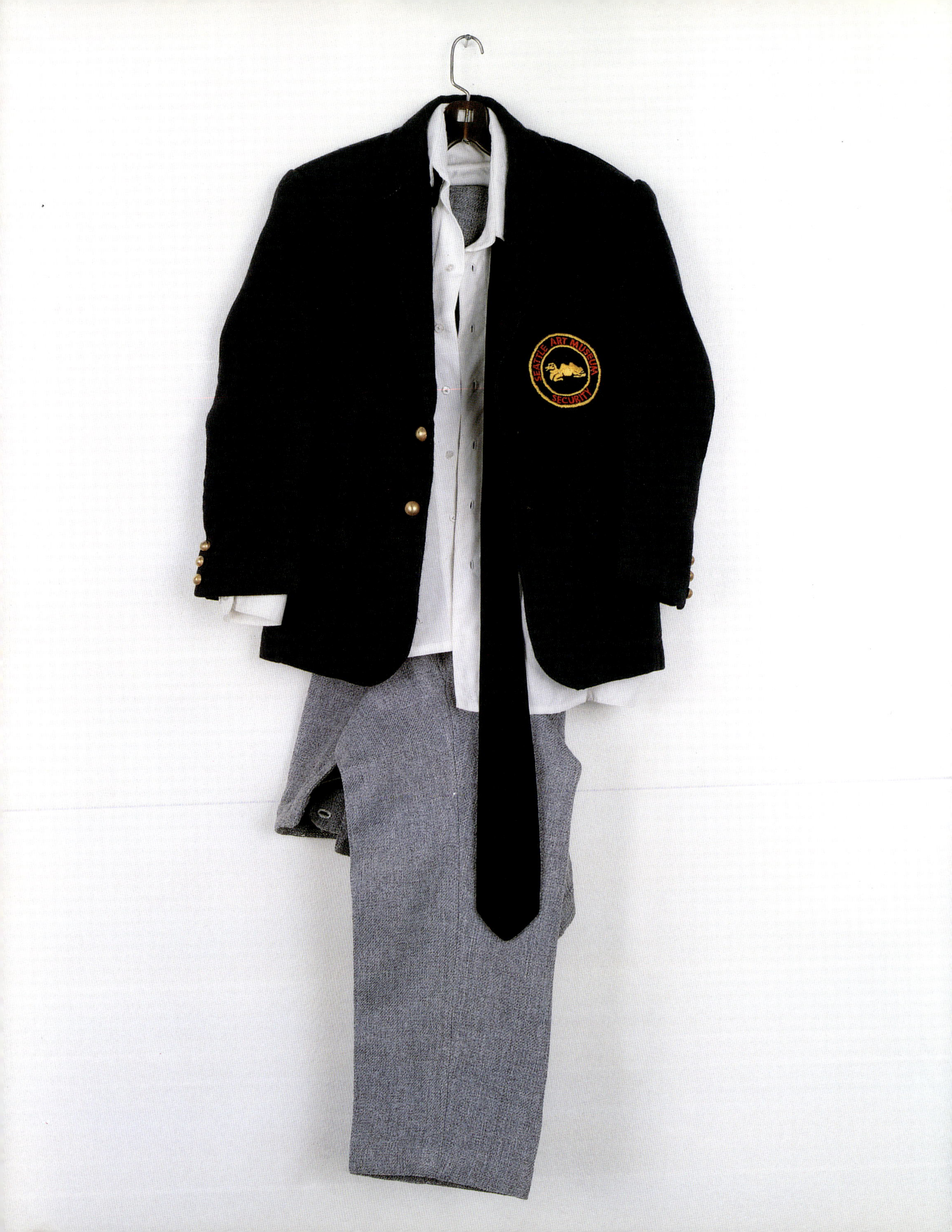
SEATTLE ART MUSEUM
SECURITY

Attention Level **Russell Ferguson**

A tiny suit of clothes, complete in every detail. A vitrine filled with thousands of hand-thrown porcelain vases. An ear of "wheat" meticulously carved from human bone. Almost everyone reacts the same way when they first encounter the work of Charles LeDray: sheer amazement that such things can be made at all. His sewing rivals that of any tailor. He can carve in wood or in bone. He can throw and glaze ceramics of the greatest delicacy. Yet, the astonishing levels of skill evident in his work have proved double-edged for LeDray. His virtuosic craftsmanship has left viewers marveling at a level of technique that has become increasingly unfamiliar in contemporary art. At the same time, though, this spectacular dexterity has, in some ways, limited the scope of the work's reception.

Even in this era of eclecticism, there is still a widespread tendency to consider artists in groups. All artists resist having their work reduced to easy categories; for LeDray, this process of classification has been particularly awkward. Essentially self-taught, apart from a couple of uncompleted classes (life drawing and gouache) at the Cornish College of the Arts, in Seattle, LeDray cannot be grouped with any particular cohort from a prominent art school, such as Yale, CalArts, or UCLA. Nor did he pay his dues as an assistant to a more established figure. Instead, he pursued a time-honored but essentially solitary form of alternative art education: He worked as a guard at the Seattle Art Museum. This form of self-education tends to seed artists' work in a particular way. The one-on-one engagement with the same works of art, day after day, can produce, in those receptive to the experience, a response that is deeply rooted in an indefinitely sustained process of looking. Attention must be held from initial impression all the way through to the most refined of details. One might think of Robert Ryman, early on a guard at the Museum of Modern Art, in New York, whose work has been a sustained meditation on the subtleties of the white monochrome. In thinking about LeDray's work, it is this aspect that I wish to emphasize: the prolonged and intense attention it seems to demand in turn from its audience.

Attention to detail, however, begins in the making of the work. LeDray had always sewn; when he moved to New York in 1989, his work consisted mostly of teddy bears, often dismembered or otherwise damaged, but often made of beautiful fabric—blue velvet, for instance. Clearly, the eighties success of Mike Kelley with (found) stuffed animals opened a space for this kind of work, despite the obvious differences in sensibility between the two artists. When LeDray began to appear in group exhibitions in the early nineties, his work often was seen in the context of responses to the AIDS crisis, a context in which his shattered bears seemed only too relevant. Works with explicitly gay references, such as *Village People* (1993) or *Pride Flag* (1996), further helped to situate the work. Thus, he was associated with artists as diverse as Nan Goldin, Felix Gonzalez-Torres, Jim Hodges, or Donald Moffett, with whom he otherwise might be difficult to group.

In many ways, however, it is best to compare him to other idiosyncratic figures who have successfully resisted assimilation into any grouping at all, such as George Ohr or H. C. Westermann. Like LeDray, both Ohr and Westermann found their highly individual voices through an intensely tactile engagement with their materials. The physical object itself always remained at the forefront of their work. In the case of Westermann, the objects he made often have been seen as responses to the trauma of his experience of combat in the Second World War. With LeDray's work, too, the suggestion of sublimated trauma often has been raised. Whether the source of any such trauma is the AIDS crisis or some earlier, perhaps childhood, experience remains unannounced. The objects themselves have to carry the whole weight of any implied meaning.

The main focus of responses to LeDray's work, however, no matter in what context it is seen, has always been the quality of its fabrication. Critics, understandably, have enthused over the jaw-dropping handiwork, but this, in turn, has tended to keep discussion revolving around questions of scale. Despite its inevitability, LeDray resists the connotations of the miniature: the cute, the whimsical, and—perhaps worst of all—the collectible. LeDray's version of the miniature can be surprisingly powerful, even violent. In *Untitled (suit with small suit cut from it)* (2000) the creation of the small version destroys the larger.

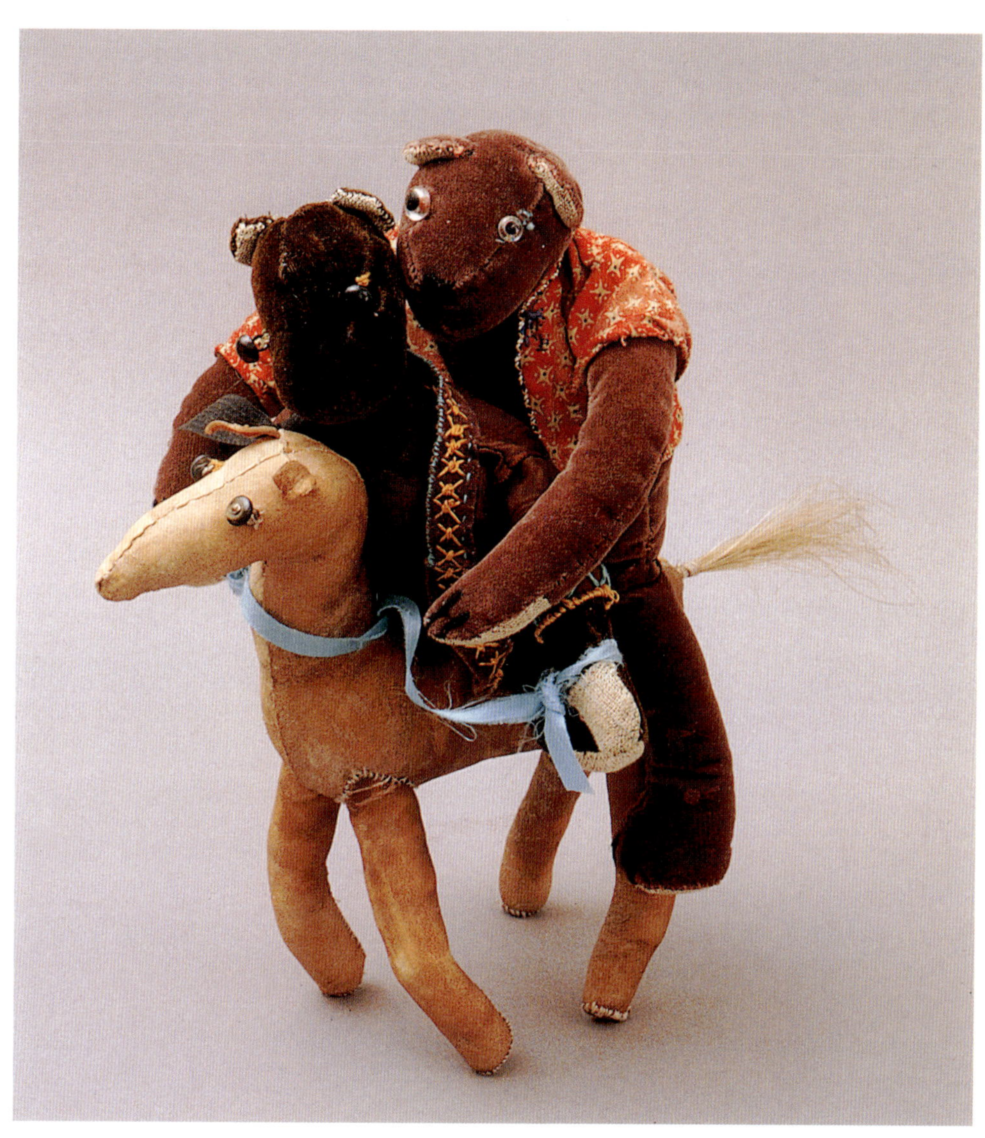

Family, 1985-88, Fabric, thread, leather, ribbon, buttons, embroidery floss, horsehair, shirt label
11 ¾ x 8 ¼ x 7 inches, Private Collection. Courtesy Sperone Westwater, New York

FOLLOWING PAGE: *Untitled (suit with small suit cut from it),* 2000, Fabric, thread, plastic, metal, wood, paint
28 ½ x 12 x 3 inches, Private Collection: San Francisco, California, Courtesy Sperone Westwater, New York, Photo: Tom Powel

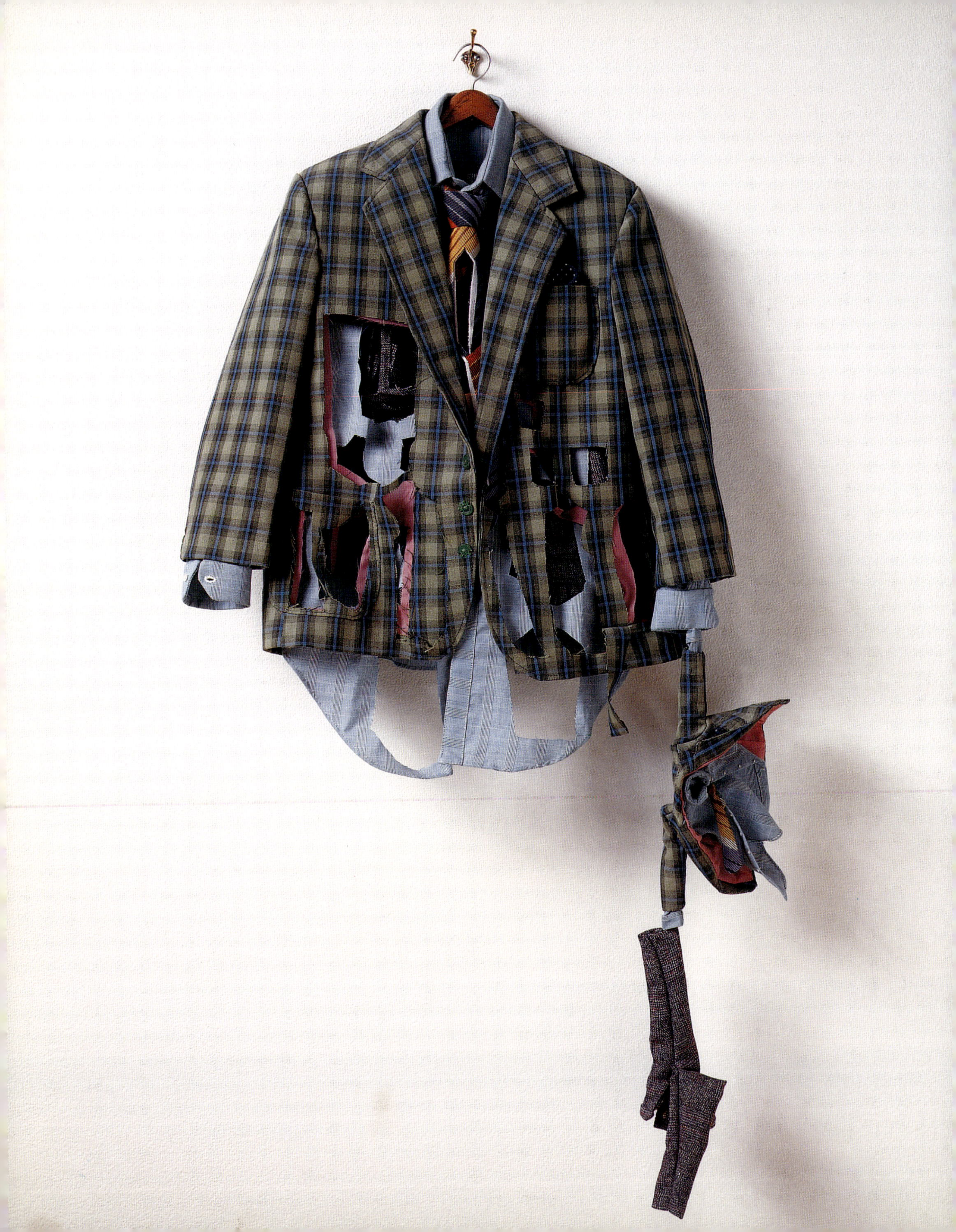

Miniature itself is a highly relative term. The models of the solar system that LeDray has constructed out of bone, for instance, do not really feel like miniatures; these planetary relationships are only ever visible to us in the form of models. Scale here does not seem a determining factor in the work, as it can, for instance, in a tiny suit of clothes. LeDray's groups of buttons, on the other hand, or his ear of wheat are, in fact, actual size. But whether a given work is a model of a vast system or a full-scale replica of an inherently small object, in both cases they tend to produce the same intense scrutiny from the viewer as do those works that adhere more closely to the conventional concept of the miniature.

One thing that LeDray has never done, however, is increase the scale of any of the objects that fascinate him, as Charles Ray has with his huge female mannequins. Large-scale tends to imply the heroic. One of the challenges that LeDray has set himself is to make work that can carry the same weight as a monumental sculpture, but without using size itself as an implied claim to significance. Monumental scale is, in itself, no guarantee against the trite. For LeDray, it is a central tenet that even work that makes use of a drastic reduction in scale should nevertheless remain a fully realized work of sculpture. If successful, it should fully manifest the ideas behind its making, regardless of size. His objects are real. Nothing is missing in them, and nothing has been lost in the process of their making.

This idea—that nothing is missing—is expressed in part precisely by the almost incredible level of detail that goes into everything LeDray makes. In 1991, he completed *workworkworkworkwork*, a large piece that comprises 588 tiny individual items. Each little detail of each tiny object exerts a certain magnetic force in its own right, but it is the cumulative effect that ultimately overwhelms the viewer. This is LeDray's way of dealing with large scale. No single object will assume a dominating position; instead, hundreds, or even thousands, of unique elements come together as their own entity.

Like *Milk and Honey* (1994–96), two thousand white porcelain vessels, each unique, shown together in a huge vitrine, *workworkworkworkwork* makes use of an accu-

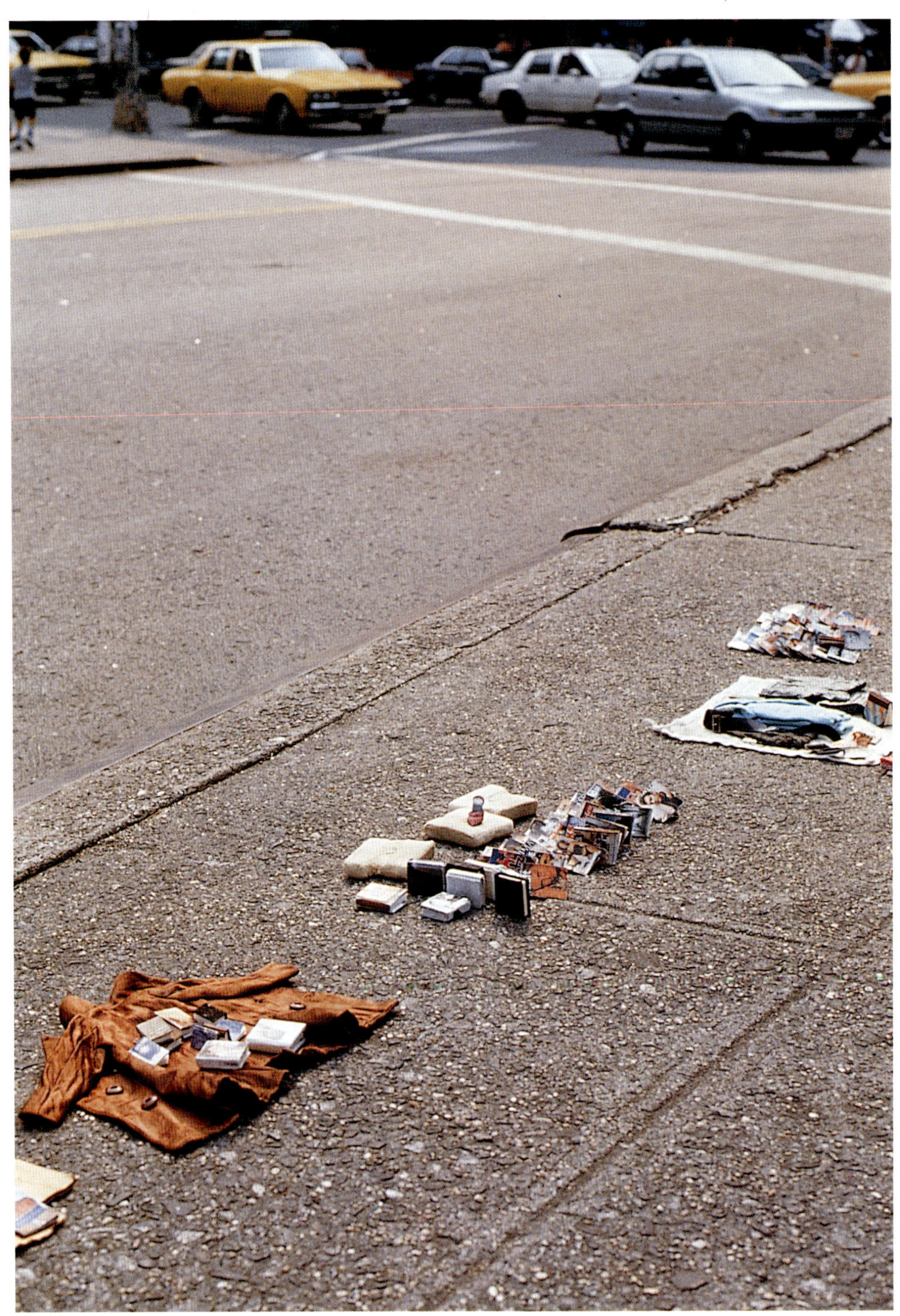

Detail, *workworkworkworkwork*, 1991, 588 mixed-media objects, Approx. 45 feet long x 10 inches wide x 2 inches deep

mulation of handmade elements to reintroduce (while still questioning) large-scale presence. Jerry Saltz has, perhaps, best caught the encyclopedic urge to completeness that characterizes it:

Not only is this a laundry bag, say—it's a laundry bag made of worn blue nylon, with a stitched in white drawstring that works; or a rock—it's a rock of "volcanic origin." A coat or dress is made of black crushed velvet and may have sewn translucent sleeves, while a lock of hair is braided, made of monkey fur, and is tied with a pretty white ribbon...

Each little book and magazine (there are 72 assorted hardcover books, 29 softcover books, and 207 assorted magazines) has individual pages that turn, with words or images on them. The suitcases have intentionally missing parts, the shoes their laces. [1]

One can feel the fascination here, the power that this work has to compel a seemingly endless attentiveness to all its details. One might think of André Breton in search of revelation at the Saint-Ouen flea market: "I go there often, searching for objects that can be found nowhere else: old-fashioned, broken, useless, almost incomprehensible, even perverse."[2] In both cases, there is a desire to make objects speak, to release their otherwise hidden meanings. The change of scale LeDray imposes upon each object contributes to their separation from their full-size context in everyday life, and acts as an invitation to contemplation. As Ralph Rugoff has written, "LeDray convinces us that tiny scale can actually concentrate an object's presence, almost in the manner of a fetish."[3]

LeDray's work tends to produce a sense of wonder that can border on disorientation. The first sign of this, perhaps, is the loss of certainty that what we are looking at is actually small. Are they really small, or just much farther away than we had at first thought? Could it be, instead, that we ourselves are actually very large? Like Gulliver, we may feel that we have traveled to a remote part of the world, somewhere quite familiar yet disturbingly strange.

This feeling of disorientation is not at all limited to size, however. Bending over to peer at an array of tiny objects, we glimpse a complete world from which we are irrevocably excluded. The uneasiness is psychological as much as it is physical. The clumsiness we feel when our bodies are juxtaposed with LeDray's perfect objects is matched by another kind of uneasiness, a sense of anomie and distance. As if the world had been carved out of brittle bone.

Joan Didion has often described this kind of blank separation from everyday things. Living in the prefigured shadow of the Manson killings, she waits for her turn. "That the time would come I never doubted, at least not in the inaccessible places of the mind where I seemed more and more to be living. So many encounters in those years were devoid of any logic save that of the dreamwork."[4] LeDray's sculpture often seems to me like a kind of dreamwork. It moves steadily, repetitively, through the raw material of the unconscious. It offers up an endless series of potentially significant signs and messages — signs that surely we are just on the verge of being able to decipher. LeDray's motifs — suits of clothes, vases, hats, and, of course, cigars—are precisely the kind of objects whose hidden meanings psychoanalysis sought endlessly to elucidate.

The clothes he makes are themselves often covered in signs of the most literal sort: Marlboro, "World's Greatest Dad," Harley Davidson, Charles. The works strain to communicate. They are very specific, although precise meanings are almost always elided. *Come Together* (1995–96) is covered in patches—peace signs, flowers, rainbows—that refer specifically to the same period in which Didion's essay was written, when LeDray was a child. They blend individual memory with a collective, generational history. Rather like the French artist Christian Boltanski, LeDray invests the trappings of unremarkable individuality with the patina of significance, calling upon his audience to look carefully at these things before they are lost forever. "It was hard to surprise me in those years," Didion writes. "It was hard to even get my attention."[5] Attention, however, is exactly what LeDray asks of us, attention to the materiality of evanescent memory.

In *Untitled* (1995) and *Torn Suit* (1997), the fabric is literally torn, frayed to the point of complete disintegration. Soon, nothing will be left. In the more overtly autobiographical *Charles* (1995), the clothes at first seem also to be torn and frayed.

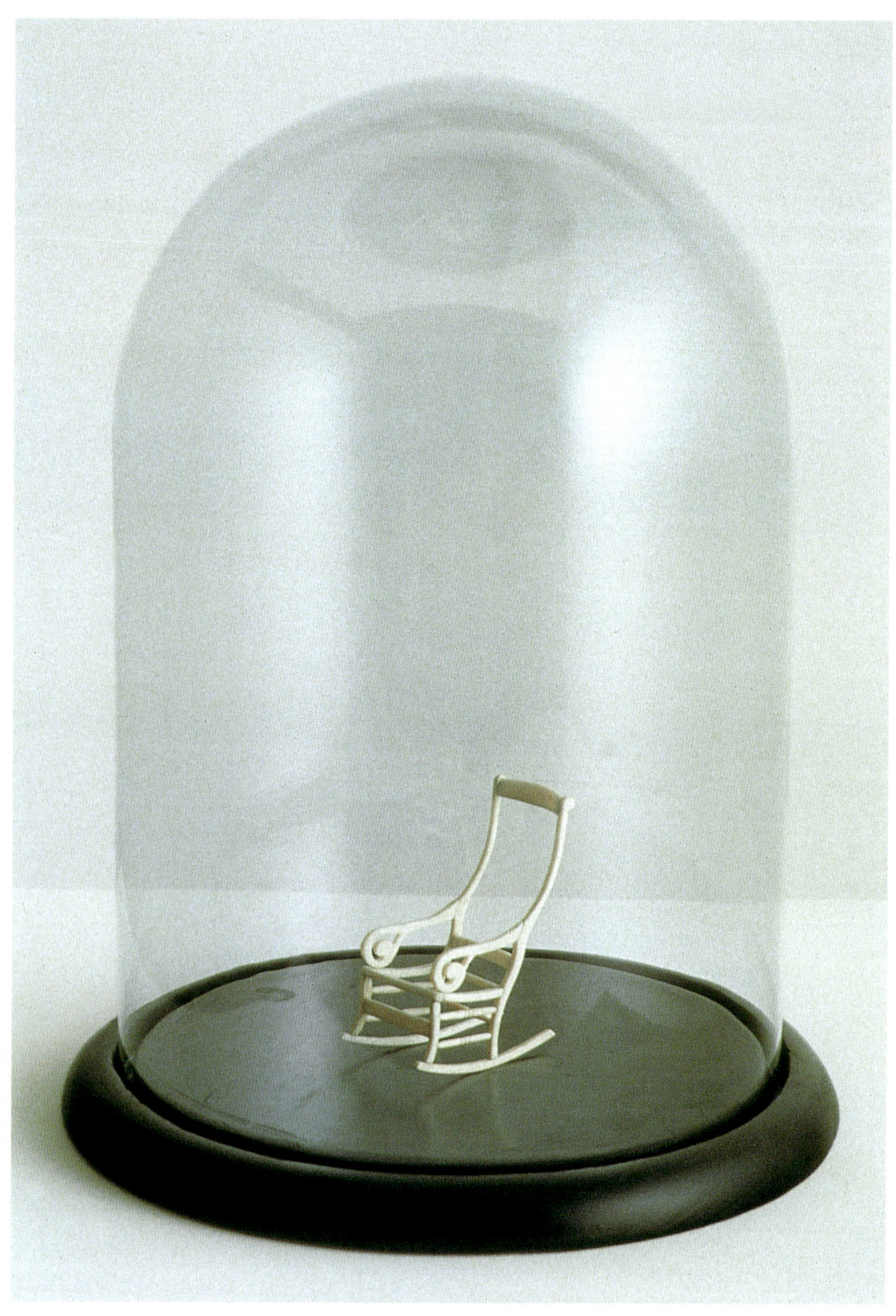

Bone Rocker, 1995, Human bone, glass, wood, 12½ x 8 inches overall
Collection: Sam and Martha Peterson, Seymor, Connecticut, Photo: Oren Slor

FOLLOWING PAGE: *Charles,* 1995, Fabric, thread, metal, plastic, paint, 19 x 14 x 4½ inches
Collection: Barbara and Leonard Kaban, Charlestown, Massachusetts

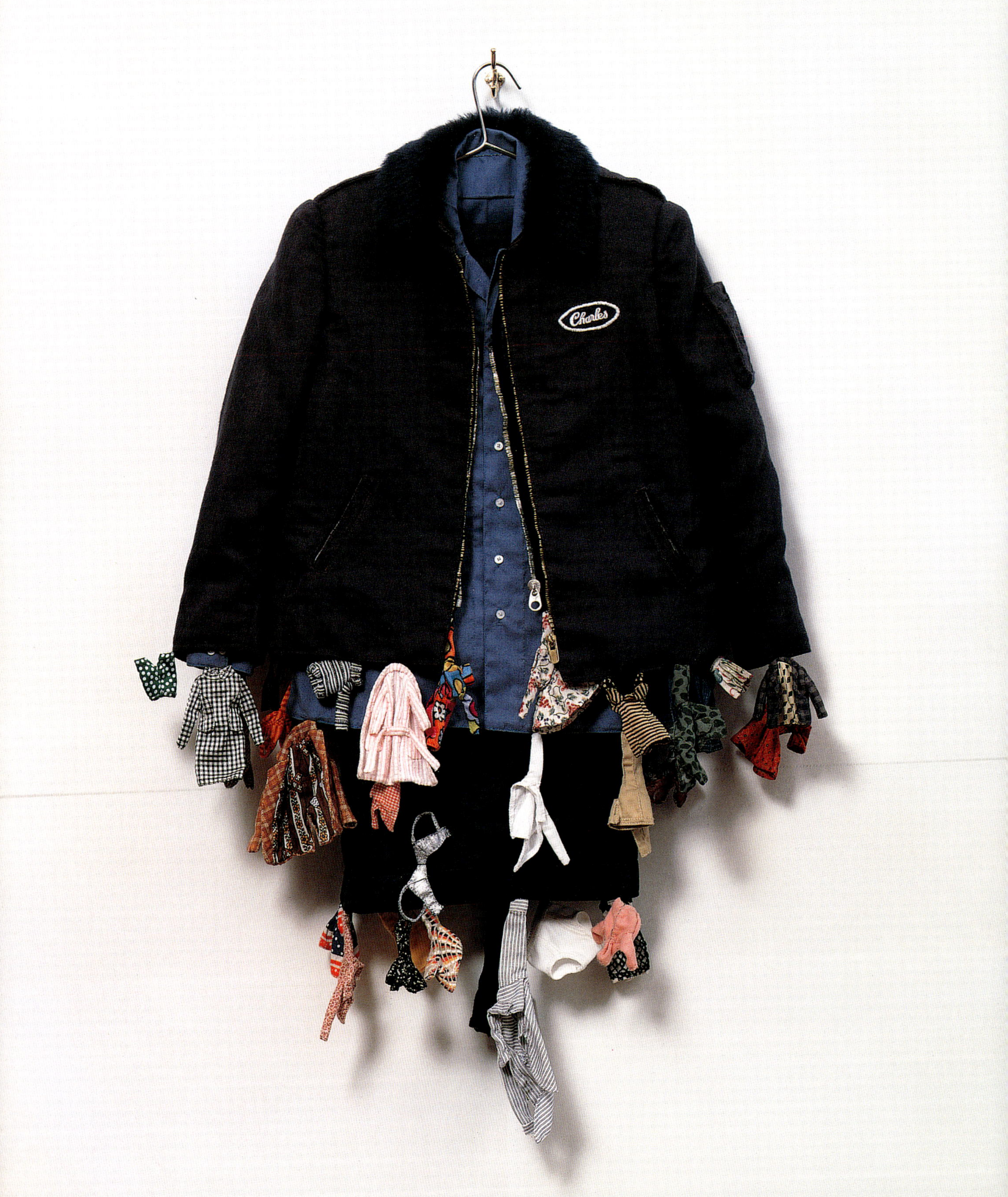
Charles

On closer examination, however, we can see that what initially appeared to be tatters are, in fact, even smaller pieces of clothing dangling from the blue work jacket with the "Charles" patch on its front. Alternative identities, in this case predominantly female, crowd in on *Charles*, pressing for their own share of attention. *Village People*'s extended row of hats suggests the camp icon's stereotypes extended indefinitely into everyday life. At one point, LeDray supported himself as a waiter, and it was at that time that he made a shabby and stained tuxedo, a piece that is simultaneously an autobiographical memento and a warning of the future should he fail as an artist. Potential futures unpursued continue to press their claims.

No physical body is ever represented as inhabiting any of LeDray's costumes. It is left to memory and the projections of the viewers of this work to fill in that absence. He provides us all the details we need to start interpreting and making judgments about, for instance, the difference between "Charles" and "Chuck." It is only the fleshy body itself that is reticently withheld.

But LeDray has also been working from the inside out, in a series of pieces carved from human bone. Like the clothing works, these sculptures avoid direct representation of the body, although they also share an intimate connection to it. The two strains are combined in the bone buttons he has been making. On one level, they are the most quotidian of objects, while on another they have something of the quality of saintly relics. Of course, LeDray's use of this most freighted of materials inevitably introduces the theme of mortality. *Bone Bed* and *Bone Rocker* (both 1996) inescapably suggest the sleep of death that lies just beyond the comfort of the bed or the rocking chair. And both, like the suits of clothes, are empty.

Is LeDray, as is often suggested, acting out an obsessive compulsion? When I visited him, his studio was filled with thousands of individually designed and thrown pots, this time polychrome, a virtual encyclopedia of ceramics on which he had already been working for two years. Consider again the 588 handmade objects in *workworkworkworkwork*. The very title suggests both obsession and compulsion. The fascination is not just for the viewer—it is clearly there for LeDray himself, both maker and observer of his own work. As Sigmund Freud wrote of his own compulsive drive to work, "A man like me cannot live without a hobby-horse, without a consuming passion, without—in Schiller's words—a tyrant. I have found one. In its service I know no limits."[6] But then, many artists are obsessive in this way. Perhaps it is a bit obsessive even to be an artist. And "obsession" is also an easy label if, like most people, you simply cannot imagine making anything remotely comparable. The evidence of such dedicated craftsmanship surprises us now. I prefer to think of LeDray as a generous artist, generous not just to the viewers of his work but also to the objects he makes. Alongside the basic compulsion to work, to produce something, runs a parallel path that seeks revelation directly in the manufacture of objects. The care, the concentrated attention, that each detail of each object receives, suggests that, rather than being a record of helpless, obsessive activity, his art is instead a cornucopia of unique items, individually attended to.

We may well marvel at the results. As we look at them in wonder, however, we may also wish to consider our own level of attention to the other objects in our world.

1 Jerry Saltz, "It Don't Come Easy," *Arts* (April 1992): 24.

2 André Breton, *Nadja* (1928), trans. Richard Howard (New York: Grove, 1960): 52.

3 Ralph Rugoff, "Little Feats," *LA Weekly* (June 21, 1996): 41.

4 Joan Didion, "The White Album," in *The White Album* (New York: Washington Square Press, 1979): 19.

5 Ibid., 20.

6 Freud, letter to Wilhelm Fleiss, May 25, 1895, in *The Complete Letters of Sigmund Freud to Wilhelm Fleiss, 1887–1904*, ed. and trans. by Jeffrey Moussaieff Masson (Cambridge: Harvard University Press, 1985): 129.

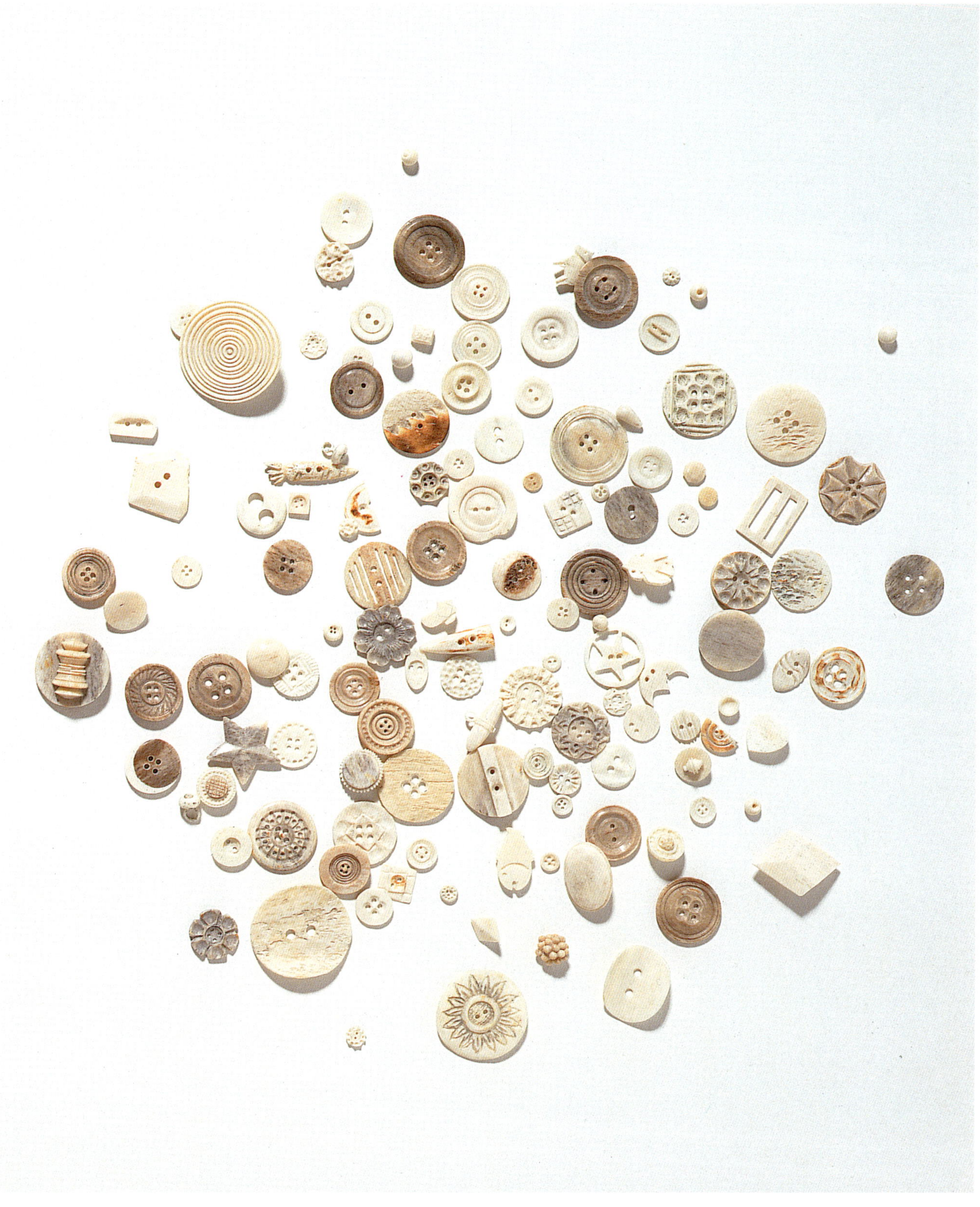

Buttons, 2000-2001, Human bone, 130 buttons, Approx. ¼ x 14 x 14 inches
Courtesy of the artist and Sperone Westwater, New York, Photo: Tom Powel

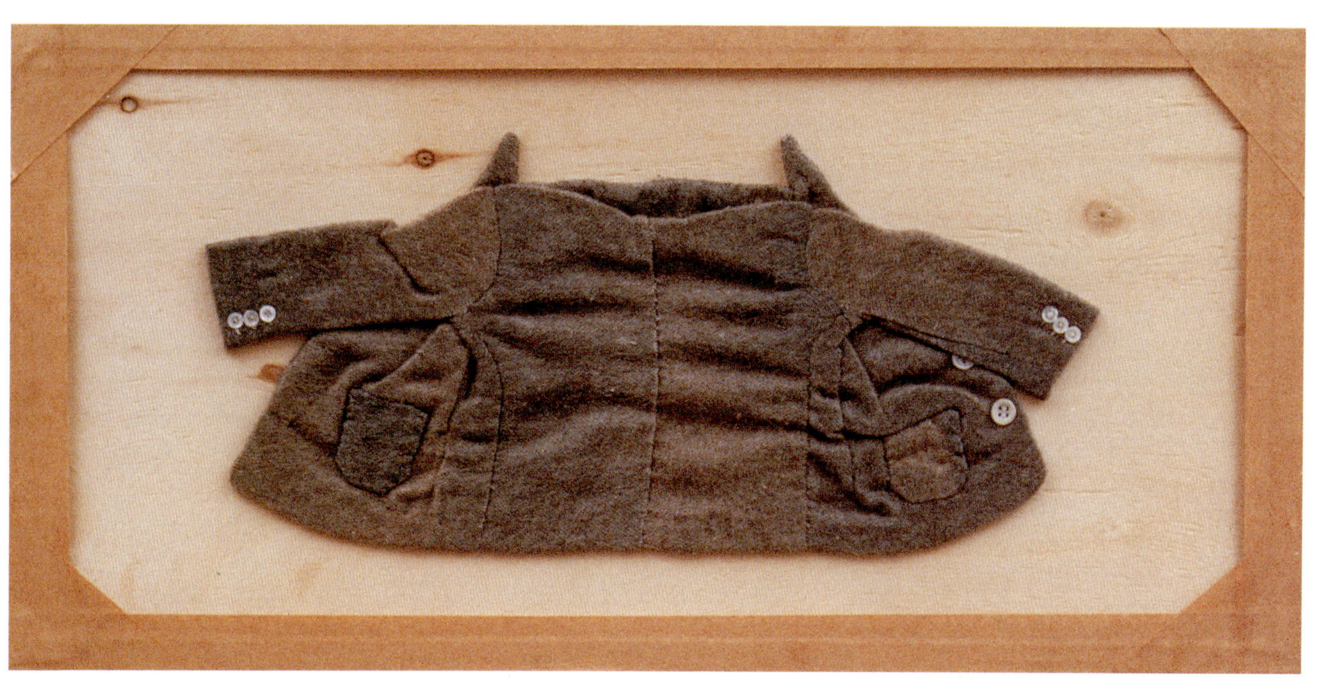

Mourning Piece, 1989, Fabric, thread, wood, glass, buttons, paper tape, 9 ¼ x 19 ¼ inches
The Carol and Arthur Goldberg Collection, New York

A Conversation between Claudia Gould and Charles LeDray

I began the interview with Charles speaking about the modesty in his art—but as the psychology of his work unfolded, I began to understand the elusive complexity of him and it: both are at once what they should and should not be. An artist who shapes human bones into astral viewing technologies (*Tellurium*, 2000) is someone removed from modest terms. I began to appreciate why Charles is an artist, who feels his work is too frequently discussed in terms of its scale and his own personal identity. Understandably, he is reluctant to answer questions that might only further contribute to such readings.

After our first interview was lost—because of a malfunctioning tape recorder—Charles' resistance strengthened into resolve. He returned to the interview process quite intrigued by the opportunity to ask me questions—to analyze, if you will, the response of a viewer to his work. Again, his approach is very informative about his own intent and vision of his art. Here follows our conversation.

Claudia Gould: *Mourning Piece* [1989], one of the earliest pieces in our show, was exhibited at the Jack Tilton Gallery in a group show called "Forbidden Games," in 1991. It was your first gallery show in New York. You were also working at the gallery, and your entry into the show was almost at the last minute.

Charles LeDray: I was the gallery's art handler. And the gallery director, Jenine Cirincione, included my piece in the show, hours before it opened.

CG: *Mourning Piece* is different in that it isn't sculptural, it isn't freestanding. In comparison to your other clothing works, it's almost like a painting laid out flat, behind glass, in an ad-hoc frame, similar to a pressed flower between glass. Its presentation has little to do with sculpture. You had also mentioned that *Mourning Piece* was made after your mother passed away. *My Hands, My Father's Hands, #2* [1991] is also pressed in the same way. It is almost as if you are enshrining them both behind glass, without breath.

CL: Perhaps they have little to do with sculpture, but they aren't paintings either.

Around the same time, I was working on *workworkworkworkwork* [1991]. It ended up containing nearly six hundred separate parts, all out of scale: books, magazines, clothes, shoes, pottery, bedding. It re-created the display of used goods for sale by homeless people on New York City sidewalks.

CG: I see *workworkworkworkwork* as being about labor. The title itself suggests the nature of your work, and the task of showing your wares on the street, like many people in New York City do, to make a living. It also has a performative element to it, but doesn't *King of the Road* [1991] as well?

CL: I wouldn't say *King of the Road* or any of my works are performance-based. In *King of the Road*, I stitched my socks and underwear where they fell. *workworkworkworkwork* was first shown on the sidewalk in Cooper Square.

CG: I've been grappling with the modesty of your work. By modesty, I'm referring to the fact that you choose things that are easily, immediately recognizable (stacks of furniture, suits, buttons). There is an understatement in the work that has nothing to do with scale—a Shaker modesty and intensity.

CL: Modesty has nothing to do with it. Modesty is as much a posture and device as being flamboyant.

CG: What do you mean by flamboyant?

CL: Look at *Come Together* [1995–96], a rainbow of tiny clothes over the outstretched arms of a hippie-embroidered work shirt.

CG: Over the top.

CL: Yes.

CG: During one of our discussions last year, you said that as a youngster you excelled at macramé, that your mom taught you to sew at the age of four. Would you say that you have come to art through craft? And how has this informed your process?

CL: When I was a kid, I loved to make things, but in my teens and twenties I wanted to make paintings. I drew and drew but never quite got the hang of painting, and in the end, I realized what I was working out on paper was more important to me than a framed canvas.

CG: So, it did inform your process in a very fundamental way?

CL: Yes, but the real magic is in the physical contact with materials—to change one thing into another.

CG: Would you say that the handmade quality of your work is in response to some of the work being produced in the mid– to late eighties?

CL: At that time, I was working as a guard at the Seattle Art Museum. There, I saw plenty of contemporary art, but also many other wonderful things.

CG: Like what?

CL: Neolithic Chinese jades, rhinoceros-horn libation cups, twelfth-century Japanese flung-ink paintings, Indian Mughal ivory powder horns, African masks, southeast Asian jewelry and textiles, and on and on. Many nights, I would leave the museum with a burning desire to make something—anything—inspired by spending the day with great works of art.

CG: I know you were exposed in Seattle to some of the abstract expressionists, such as Clyfford Still and Jackson Pollock. Are there references in your work to these artists in, say, *Dilettante* [1994] and *Torn Suit* [1997–98]? Do you see these works as homages to these artists and movements? Are you trying to feel closer, more aligned to them in your work?

CL: *Torn Suit* is a simple exercise in adding and subtracting materials. I built an entire suit of clothes, right down to the shoulder pads and hand-serged seams, and then I removed almost half of it with scissors and sandpaper. And *Dilettante* is not a homage to abstraction.

CG: Do you want to ask me a question?

King of the Road, 1991
Underwear, found
quilt, buttons
74½ x 54¼ inches
Collection: Walter Sudol
and Steven Johnson,
New York
Photo: Beth Wessen

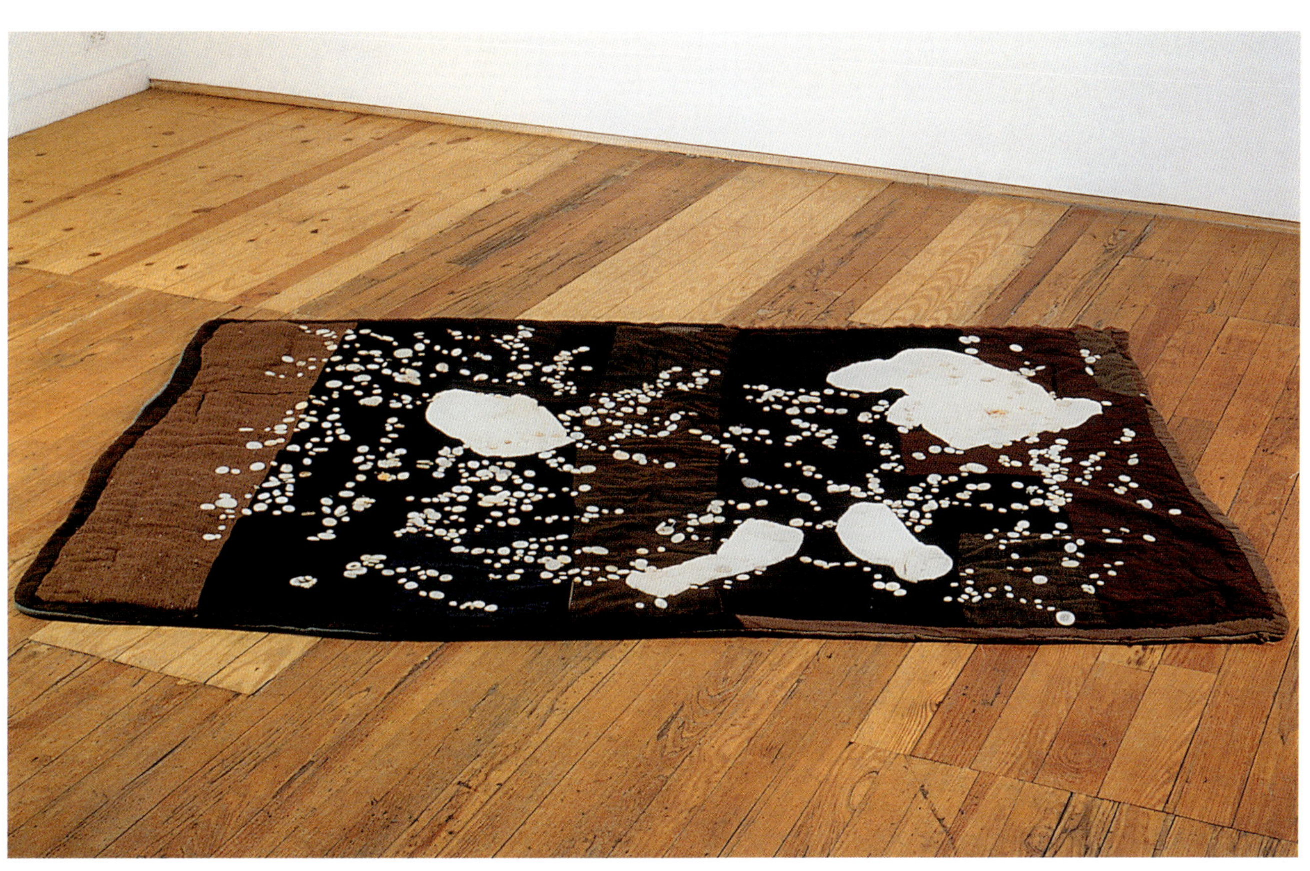

CL: You mentioned that you first saw my work at the Tom Cugliani Gallery in 1993; what do you remember of it?

CG: Certainly, I remember going into this show and being completely blown away. I remember being drawn into the work, and as Russell [Ferguson] says, Your mouth drops open at how everything is handmade. In the late eighties and early nineties a lot of work was manufactured outside the studio; yours was a refreshing departure from that. There was an uneasiness; I didn't know what to make of it. It didn't make me very comfortable, yet they were all familiar things . . . a loss of innocence, perhaps? It must have unnerved me, made me think of personal things.

CL: Okay, you also saw my 1996 show at Jay Gorney Modern Art. Did you have a similar impression?

CG: Yes. I think you were diversifying your materials, though. You were going in another direction, taking the same similar ideas but using different materials. I don't remember any bone materials at all in your previous show. I remember clothing and bears.

I was also interested in the whole deconstructive notion in fashion, since I look at clothing and I follow fashion a lot. In the early nineties, seeing these bears—eyeless, limbless—made me think of looking at the Japanese designers, who made clothes with three legs or three arms, or one arm missing, with holes under the arms. I know your interests do not lie here, but this is what I thought of at the time.

CL: You saw it as fashion?

CG: No [laughs]. But I was really interested in these dismembered bears, which looked as though they had gone through a war.

CL: So, you see that work as the product of violence?

CG: I saw it as a brutal act, but also a very gentle one. . . but that's where the confusion lies—that certain innocence. I saw them as something gone awry.

They weren't mangled; it's not as though a dog came along and chewed up one of them. The remains were all intact. There was something perfect about their imperfection. The clothing pieces. . . something is imperfect about this piece that is so small. Something doesn't work. There is something always off, and I think that's the uneasiness that I feel.

CL: How did you feel when you first saw my bone work?

CG: I didn't know it was bone.

CL: How did you find out?

CG: I read the label [laughs].

CL: What did you think it was made of?

CG: Ivory, I thought it was ivory, which is a bone, but it's not human bone. I found it completely piercing, going to the core of our own anxiety. When I look at stuff, I don't think about the rest of the world, I think about how it may affect me. It's really hard for me to say, "Oh, well, this is about the war and obstruction of humanity—building art out of the remains of the human spirit." I don't look at it like that. I saw it like a knife going through you. For me, it was really much more like a knife. It was painful, yet you're looking at these pieces and there is nothing painful about them.

There is a certain banality to them, which I really like. And this is why I'm attracted to Shaker furniture, because I really love this pure, basic, stripped-of-everything appearance of the furniture. At the same time, you also reference Victorian and European Modern styles, all made exquisitely from bone, which is where the paradox lies.

CL: I've always been attracted to ivory, but I can't make a personal connection with it as an art-making material. Human bone, on the other hand, has its own challenges. Given your comments on the subject so far, do you feel the same about my sculpture *Wheat* [2000]?

My Hands,
My Father's Hands, #2, 1991
Cotton, wood, thread,
mother of pearl,
paper tape, glass
12 x 9 inches
Collection: Ruth &
Jake Bloom,
Marina del Rey, California

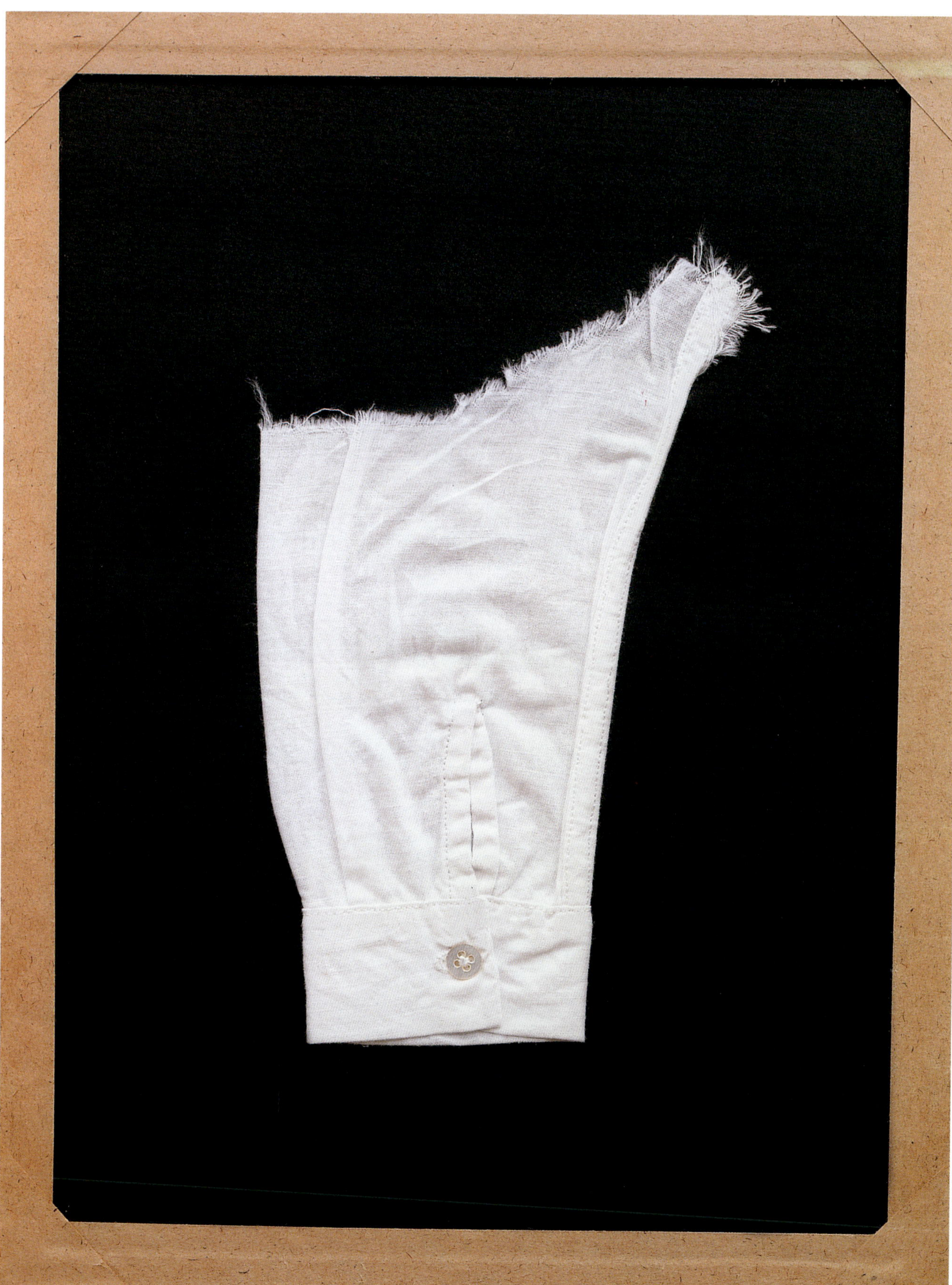

CG: I haven't quite figured out *Wheat*, and I was hoping you could help me with that. If you want, you can see it is as the basis of what people in the world eat. It's used to make bread, our food base—yet, it's this delicate flower. Can you talk to me about *Wheat*?

CL: I think you described it quite beautifully.

CG: I don't see how it fits in with a lot of the other things you do. . . nature. For instance, *Buttons* [2000–2002] and *Door* [1999] have to do with opening and closing; they have very similar meanings—they're also about protection or access. Whereas *Wheat*. . . I don't know, I have to turn it back to you.

CL: Do you think the use of human bone as an art material is immoral?

CG: That would never play into my thoughts. Do you feel it is immoral?

CL: No, I was just curious about your comments on your first impression that it was "like a knife going through you."

CG: No, no, no, it's really more personally shocking. And then you think, "My God, where did he get the bone?" I know other people are curious about this, too.

CL: Would you share your feelings about *Door*?

CG: Well, it's sitting there by itself, similar to other work, such as *Tellurian* [2000]—but the door is just laid out flat.

CL: Is it laying flat?

CG: Isn't it? Isn't the door just straight down?

CL: Well, it has a doorknob, which prevents it from lying flush to the ground.

CG: *Door* is claustrophobic to me. You envision that there is a cellar downstairs, and I think of Robert Gober's work at the last Venice Biennale—that suburban panic of trying to get out. This door has that feeling of a childhood door, as though you're being locked in a room.

But I have another question for you: Why are you so reluctant to talk about your work?

CL: It's not for me to say what it is or means. It exists on its own, for better or worse, outside of me.

CG: Okay, would you prefer to ask me more questions?

CL: Of the work in the show is there one piece that you're more drawn to or repelled by?

CG: You know, it's funny—the minute you say that I think about *Untitled/Mattress* [1993], because I love the story of how you made it, the process of burning it in the microwave oven. The soiled mattress makes me think of a child wetting his or her own bed, or about a girl having her period, stains from sex, etc.; it can be about guilt and shame. All those types of things inform me when I look at this mattress that's been soiled. Life has been lived on the bed, and it tells a universal story of life. Although I can't say that's my favorite piece. When you asked me that question, this came to my head: I like *Charles* [1995] and *Untitled (Broken bear)* [1993], and, of course, *Pretty Teacher* [1993], which I see as being about self-pleasure.

CL: At the time I created them, I saw *Untitled/Mattress*, and *Pretty Teacher* as a kind of balancing act. *Untitled/Mattress* has a sense of history; *Pretty Teacher* is all about freedom.

Another question: How, then, do you relate to a piece like *Milk and Honey* [1994-96]?

CG: I see *Milk and Honey* as plentiful, full of life, and very cheerful, clean. The title of it alone is about purity and just nurturing. With a multitude of pieces, there's a kind of humor combined with awe. There's more lightness to it—hope and the future.

CL: How do you think it fits in with the other work?

Untitled (Bear with one leg), 1992
Velvet, cotton, thread, wire
11 x 5 x 4 inches
Private Collection
Photo: Beth Wessen

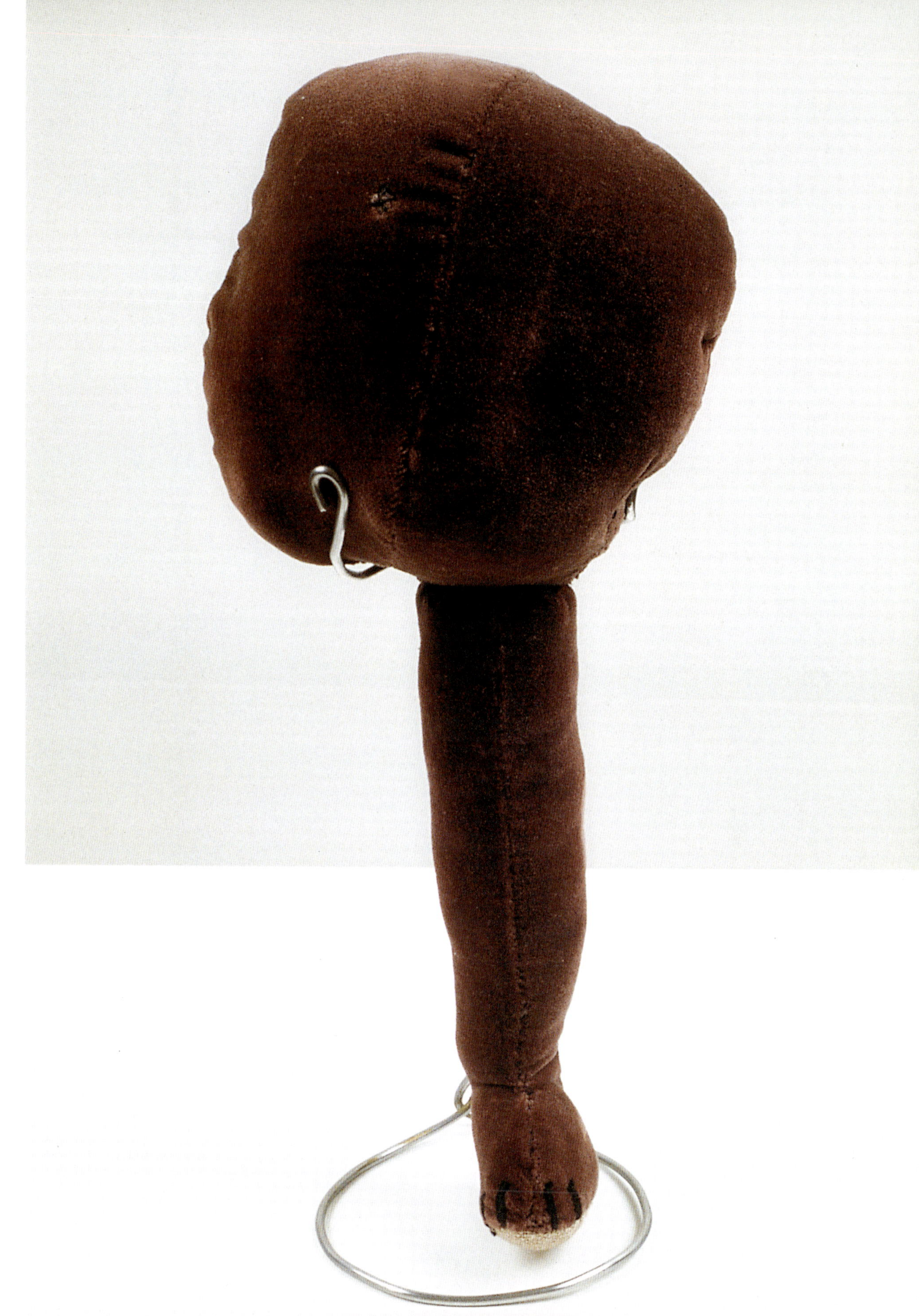

CG: They make perfect sense. First of all, you're dealing with objects that are everyday: clothing, pots, jars, wheat, furniture, a door. So, looking at it as an entire picture makes perfect sense. I know you do not like the "obsessive" word, but making X amount of vessels by hand is, is. . .

CL: Would you call a piece like *Field for the British Isles* [1993], by Anthony Gormley, with its thirty-thousand figures, obsessive?

CG: Oh, yes, completely obsessive. But what about your interest in ceramics?

CL: I saw a lot of ceramic art in Seattle in the sixties and seventies. Nothing is more immediate or primal than clay.

Would you talk about *Charles*?

CG: I assumed it was a self-portrait, mirroring the kind of blue-collar work clothes you wear every day. It reminded me of *wide boys*, a term used in England for people who sell their wares—stolen or not—on the street. They open their jacket, and inside are watches, pins, all kinds of jewelry they have to sell. You were also turning yourself inside out, your guts coming out, dangling on strings. At the same time, it could also connote offspring. I thought it was a work about vulnerability, showing you to the world, opening yourself to the elements.

CL: Russell talks about the small scale of much of my work as "just much farther away than we had at first thought." Do you feel the same way?

CG: What I found particularly noteworthy in Russell's essay is the disorientation that comes from looking at your work. You become disoriented and you end up questioning yourself: "Am I small? Am I large?" You question yourself about your own identity. Furthermore, you're not exactly sure what is normal or not normal, wrong or right. I thought he talked about that very eloquently. If that's what you're referring to. . . I agree with him; I think he hit on something for me that I wasn't able to articulate. Of course, it changes from piece to piece. For instance, *Wheat*, or *Buttons*, they are actual size; in *Tellurian*, size becomes another issue.

CL: All my work is the actual size it needs to be.

CG: How do you feel about seeing much of your work over the last decade in one place?

CL: A lot of this work I haven't seen in years. It's a great opportunity for me to reexamine my life and work.

CG: *Village People* is an ongoing project that you have been working on for about ten years; it includes more than one hundred workers' hats from different walks of life. I think of the rock band, and their performance costumes (their work clothes); of the eclectic population of Manhattan's Village; of the world as a village, a self-portrait, and portraits for all of us, but in these roles. . . Holland Cotter [*The New York Times*, May 1994] says it best, that *Village People* "offers personal history as a cavalcade of headgear for men, from a propeller beanie to a crown to a black leather motorcycle cap. . . the hats are both absurd (a little boy's wildest macho fantasies come true) and sad (the hats are hung high on the wall, out of reach and unworn), and point up nostalgia's attraction while keeping it at arm's length." What does this say about contemporary identities?

CL: It's all drag isn't it?

Untitled (Bear in a corset box), 1989
Velvet, buttons, wood, paper, fabric, nails, brassiere box
11 ¾ x 5 ¼ x 3 ¼ inches
Private Collection, New York

FOLLOWING PAGE:
Untitled, 1989
Papier maché, glass, thread, fabric, sawdust, buttons, wax pins, needles
Variable dimensions
Private Collection
Courtesy Sperone Westwater, New York

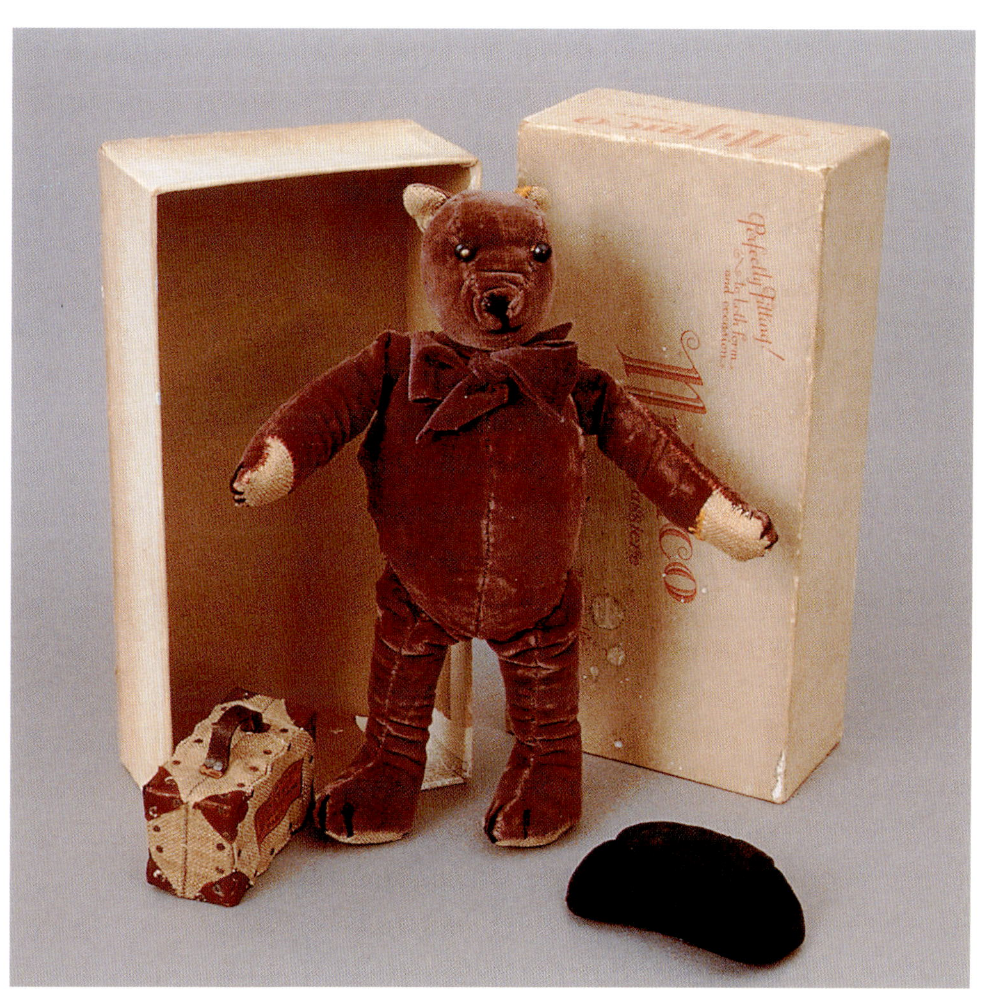
Perfectly Fitting!
to both form
and occasion.

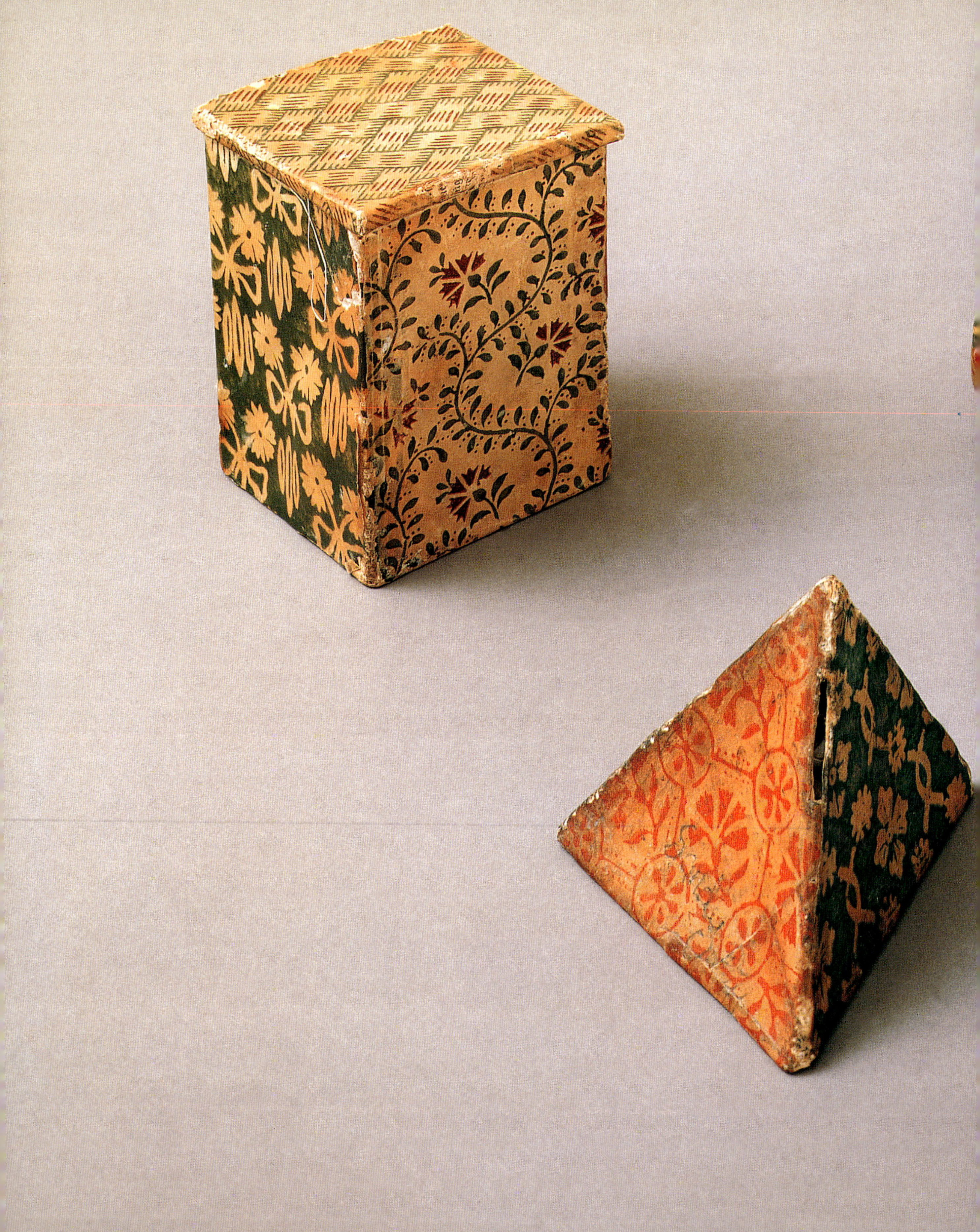

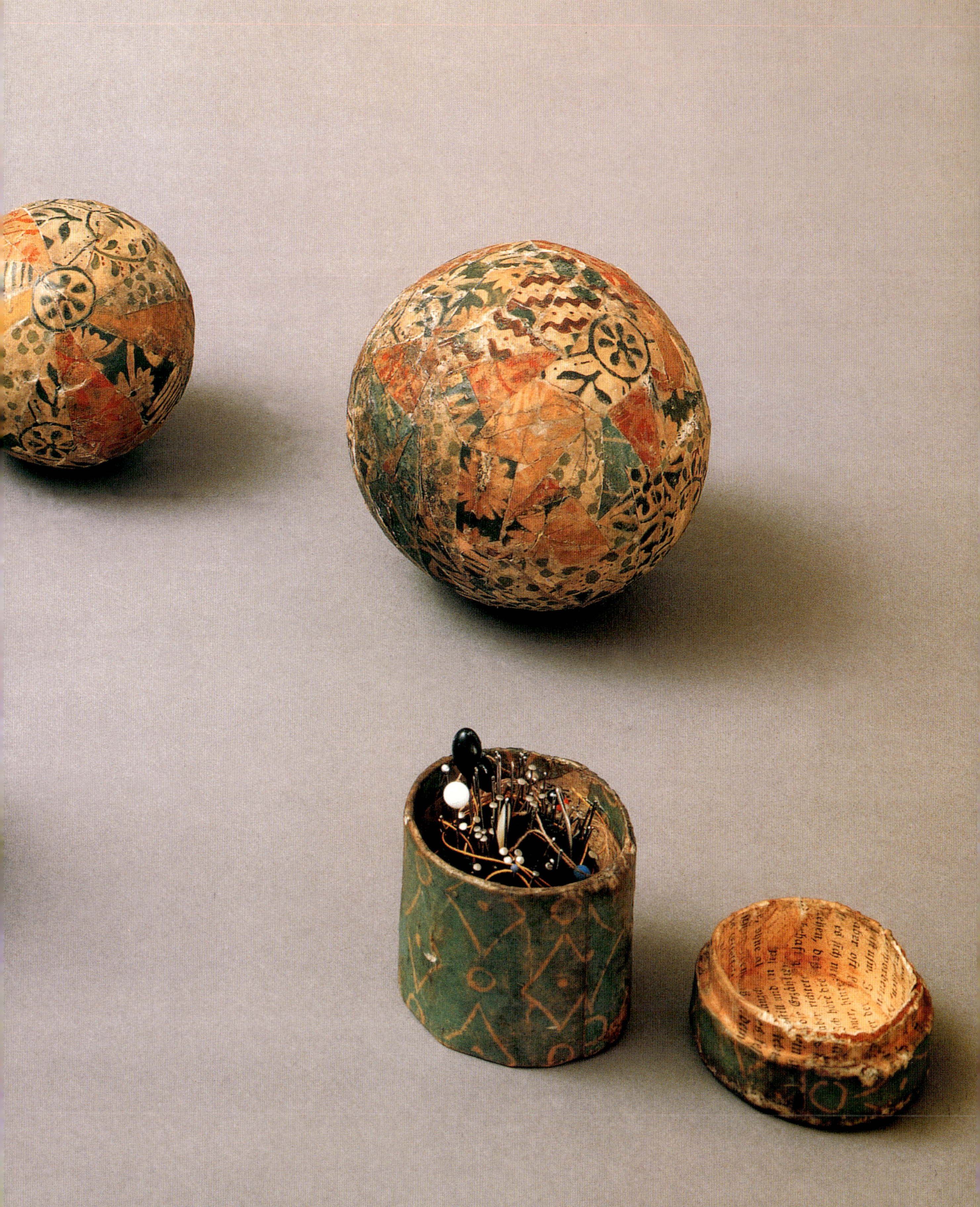

Untitled (Tar bear), 1991
Tar, velvet, buttons, thread,
sawdust, sugar, porcelain
14 ½ x 20 x 4 inches
Collection: Ralph Balass,
New York

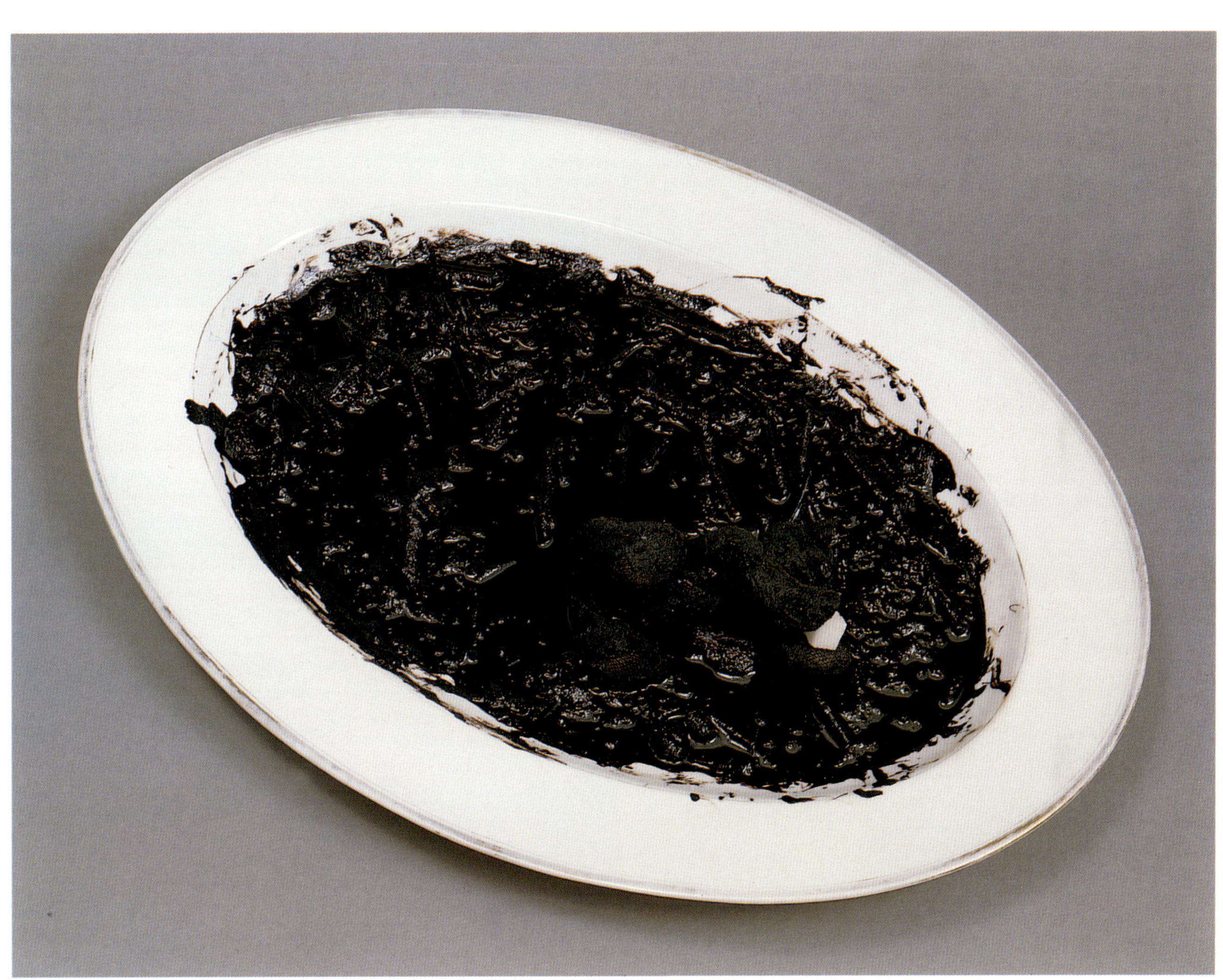

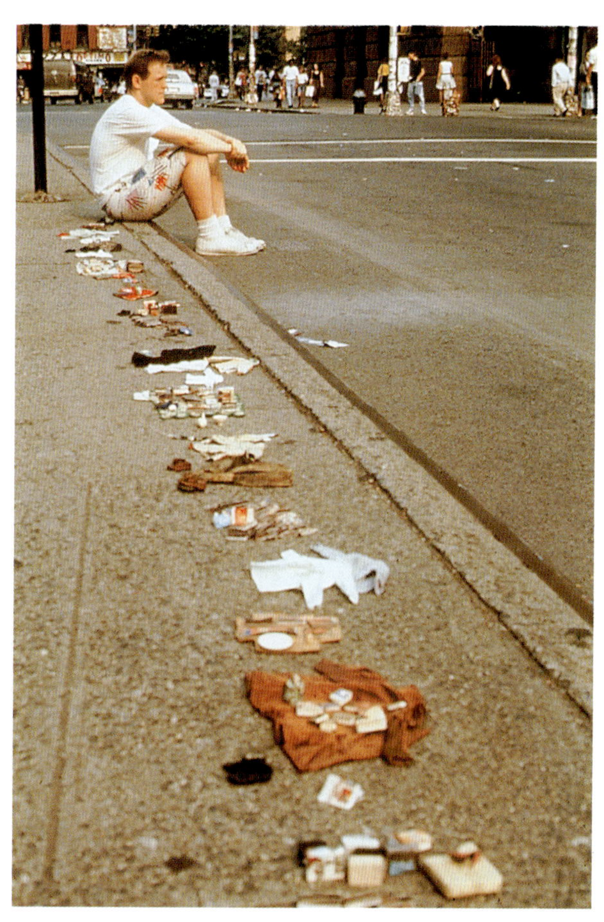

workworkworkworkwork, 1991, 588 mixed-media objects, Approx. 45 feet long x 10 inches wide x 2 inches deep
Collection: Robert J. Shiffler Foundation, Greenville, Ohio

Becoming/Mister Man, 1992
Fabric, thread, wire
14 x 12 ½ x 4 ¼ inches
Private Collection, New York
Photo: Beth Wessen

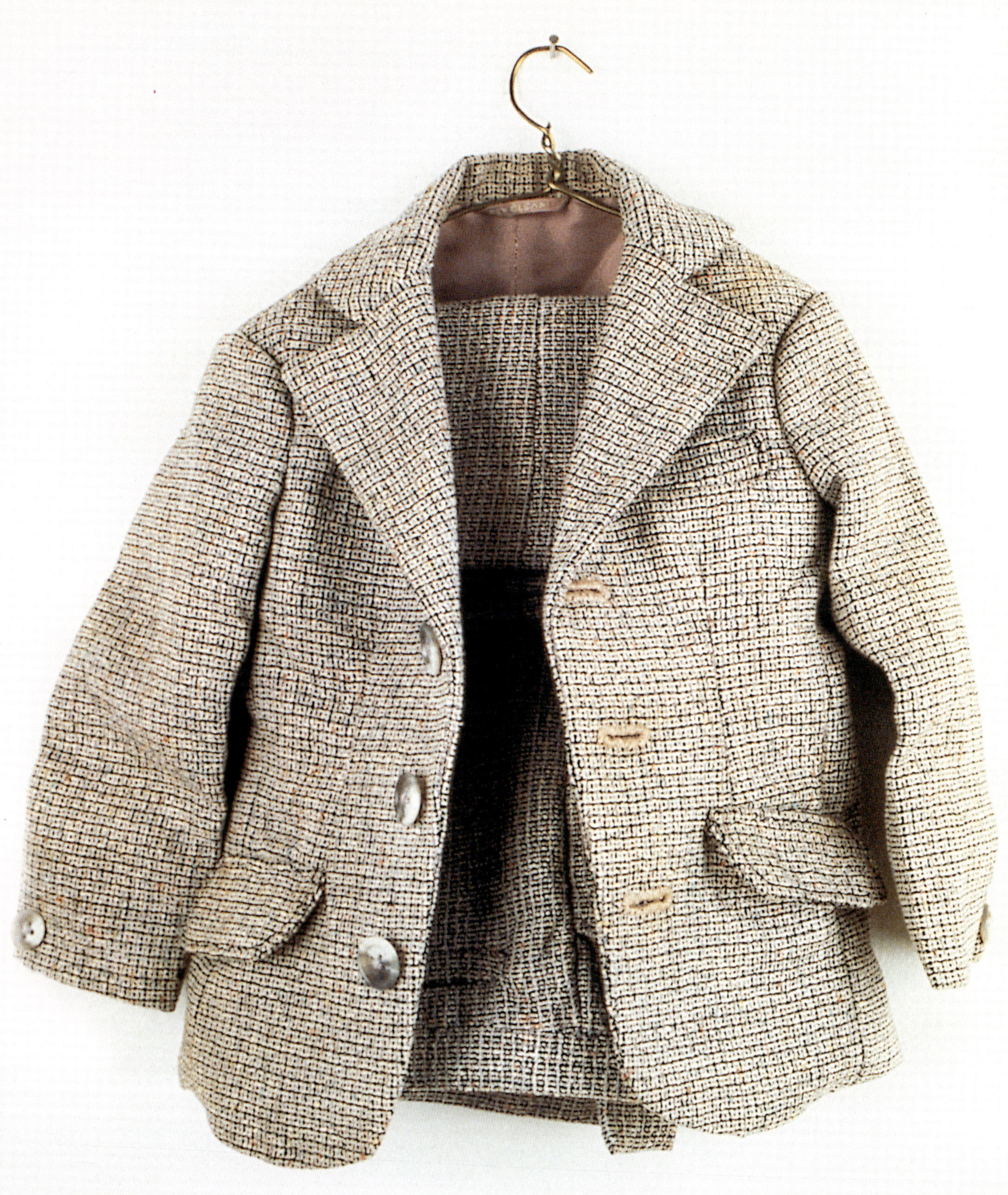

Untitled (Broken bear), 1993
Leather, cotton, thread
5 [illegible] x 3 [illegible] x 1 [illegible] inches
Collection: Kenneth L. Freed,
Boston

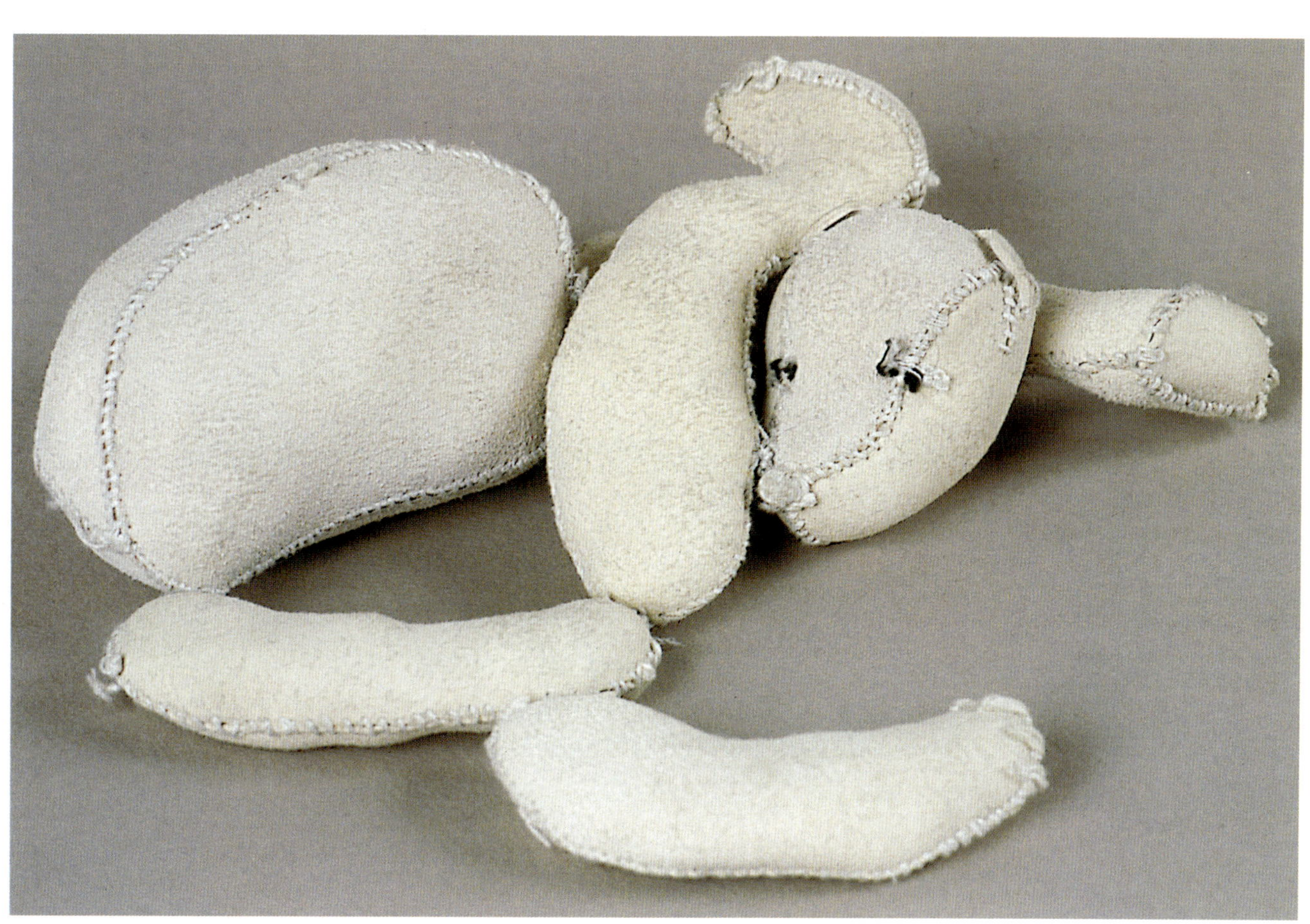

Untitled/Clothesline, 1993
Fabric, thread, buttons
34 feet x 3½ inches x 5 inches
Collection: Susan and
Michael Hort, New York
Photo: Jean Brasilla/
Villa Arson

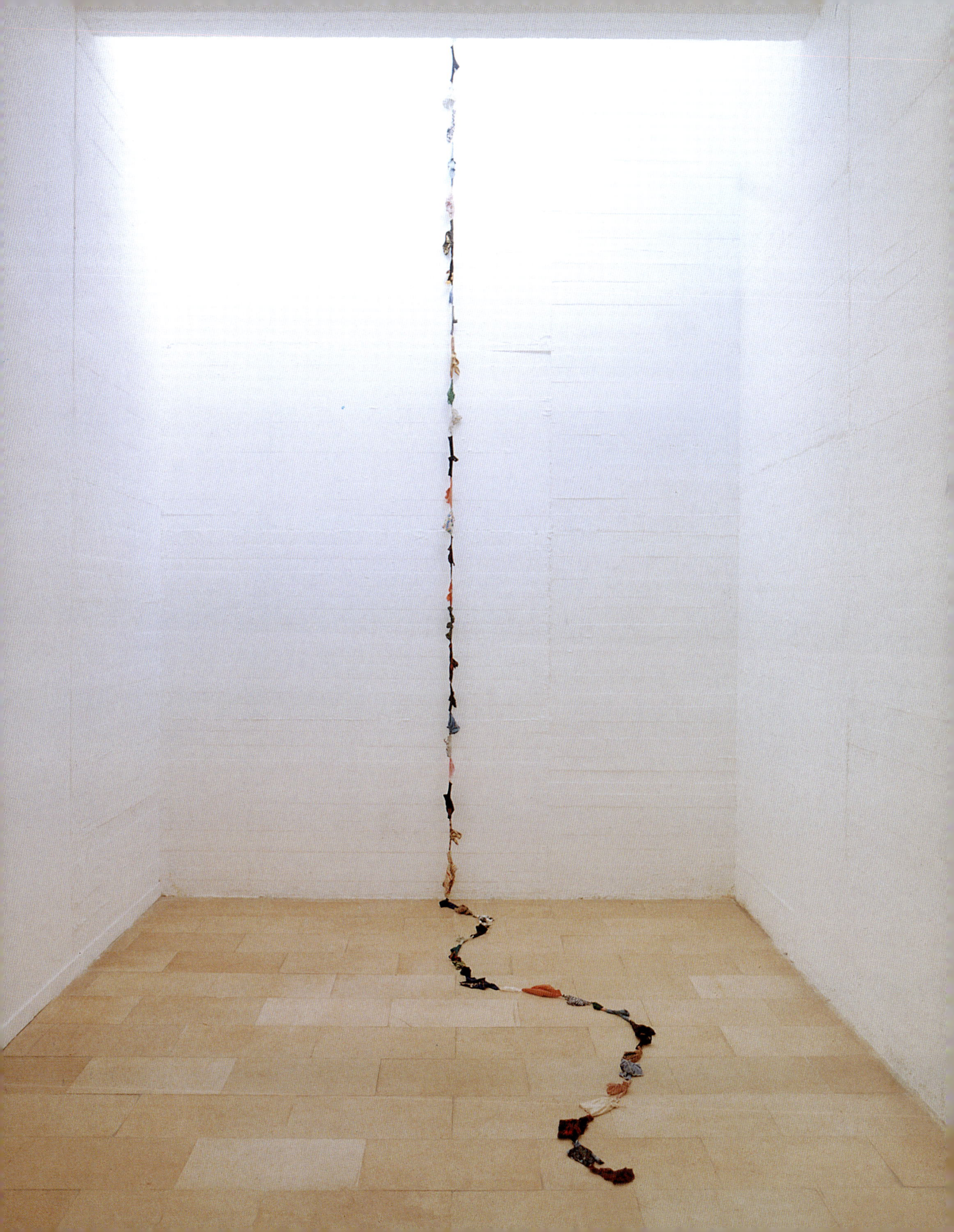

Untitled/Web, 1992
Fabric, thread, yarn, buttons
82 x 55 x 5¼ inches
Collection of Penny
and David McCall
Foundation, New York
Photo: Beth Wessen

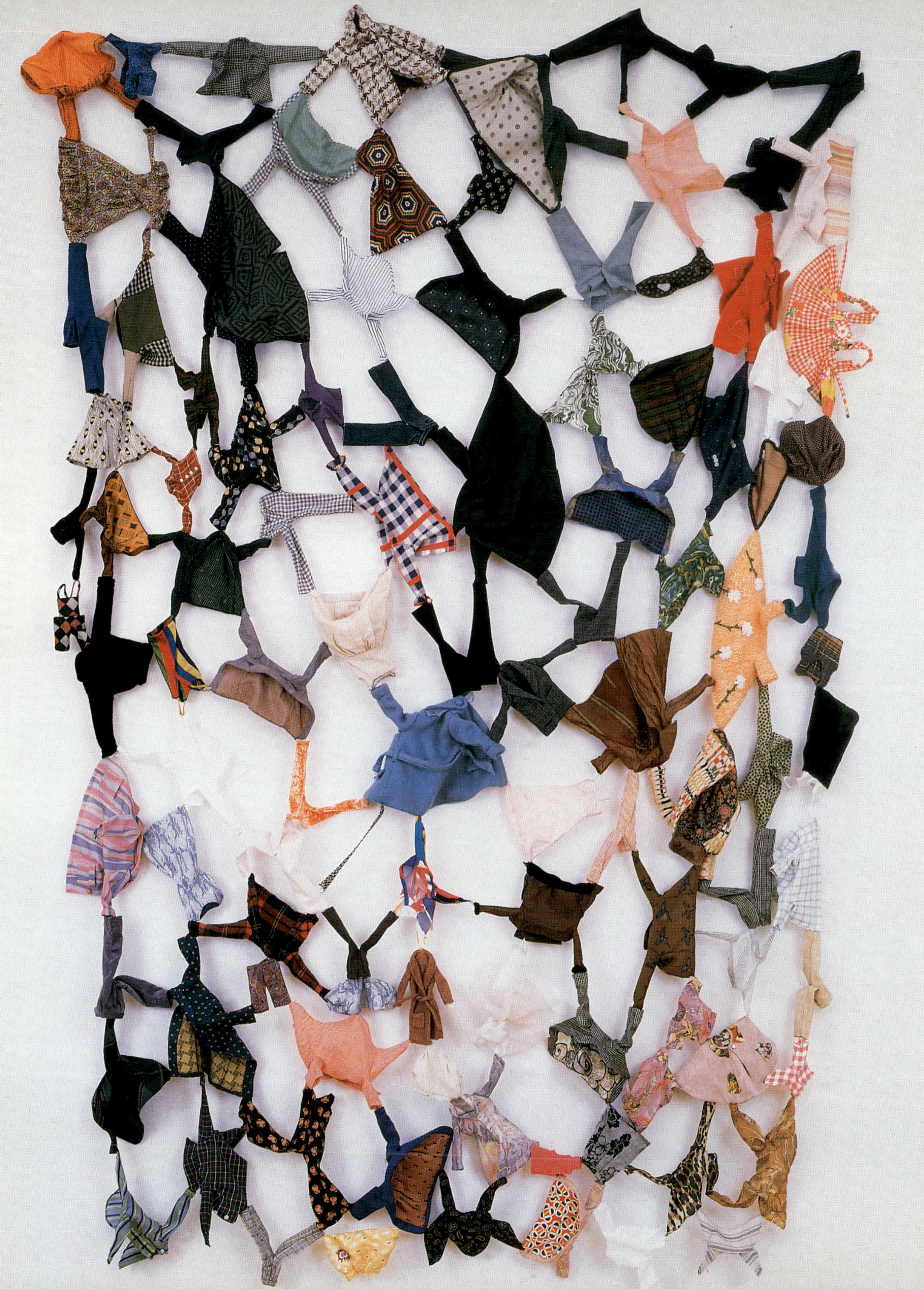

Dilettante, 1994
Fabric, thread, wood,
metal, paint,
mother of pearl, leather
17 ¼ x 12 x 4 ¾ inches
Private Collection

FOLLOWING PAGE:
Collecting Teeth, 1993
Porcelain, fabric, thread
¼ x 12 x 12 inches
Private Collection
Courtesy Sperone Westwater,
New York

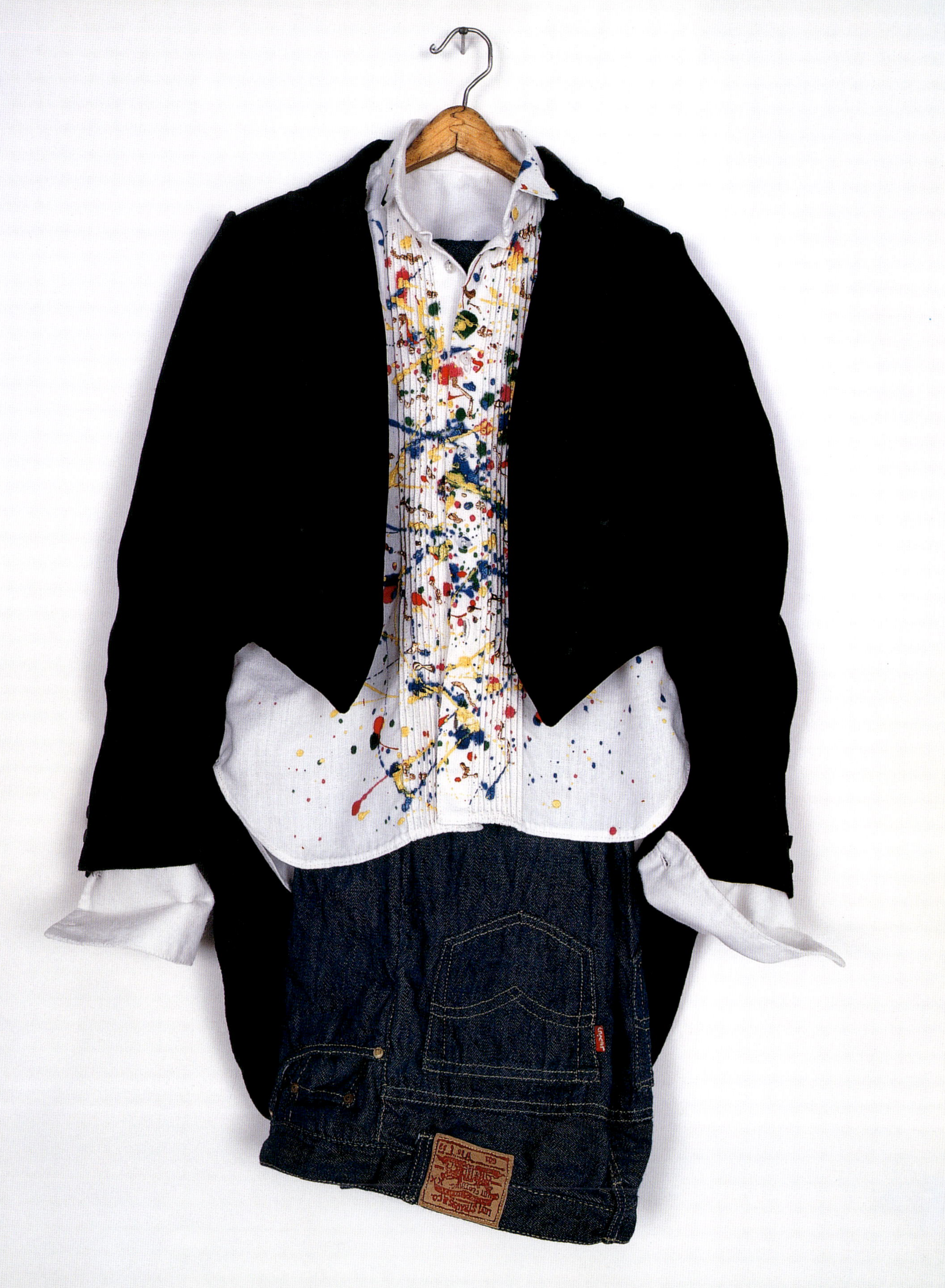

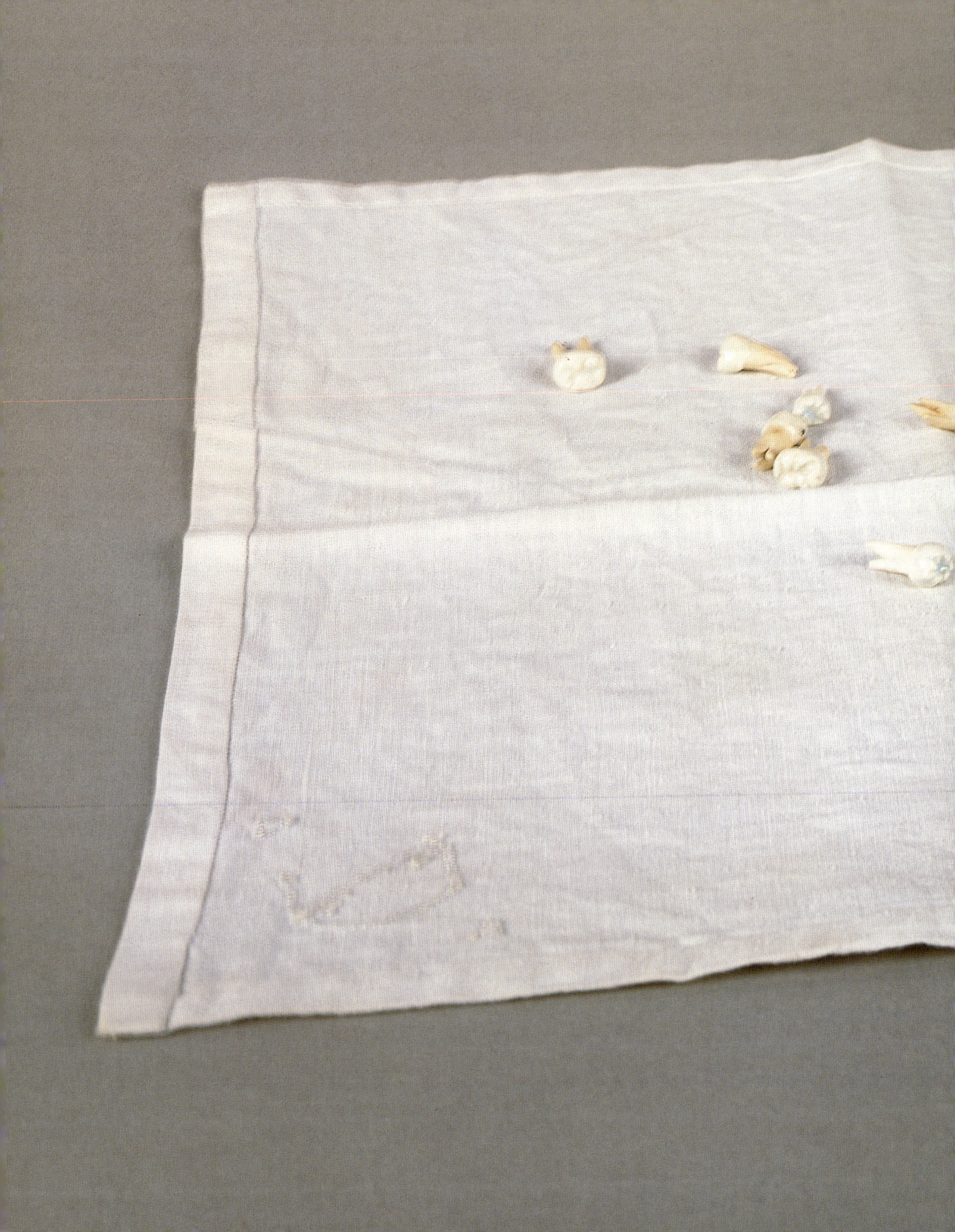

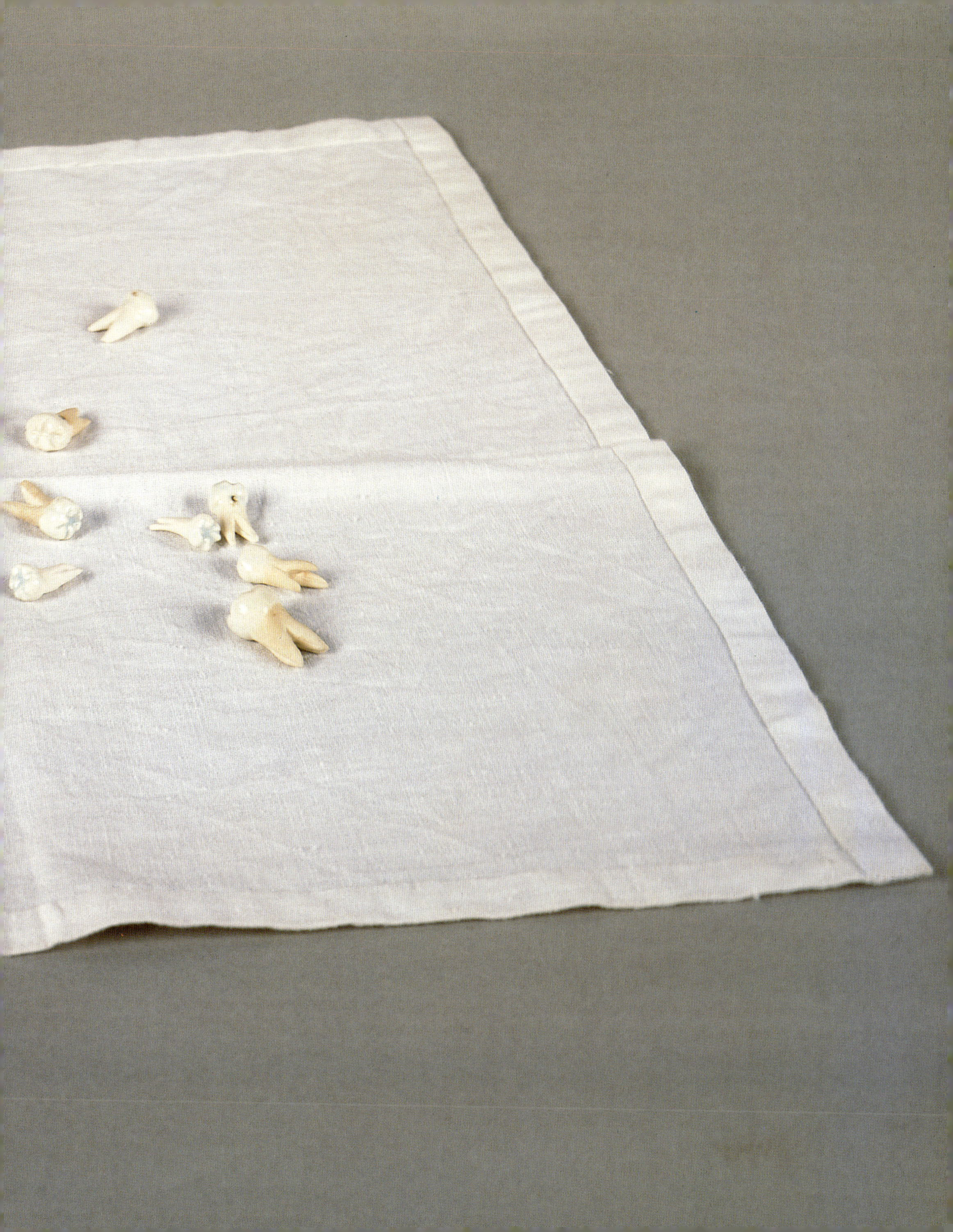

Pretty Teacher, 1993
Fabric, wire, thread, cotton
15 ¾ x 12 ½ x 8 ¼ inches
Private Collection
Courtesy of
Sperone Westwater, New York
Photo: Jean Brasilla/
Villa Arson

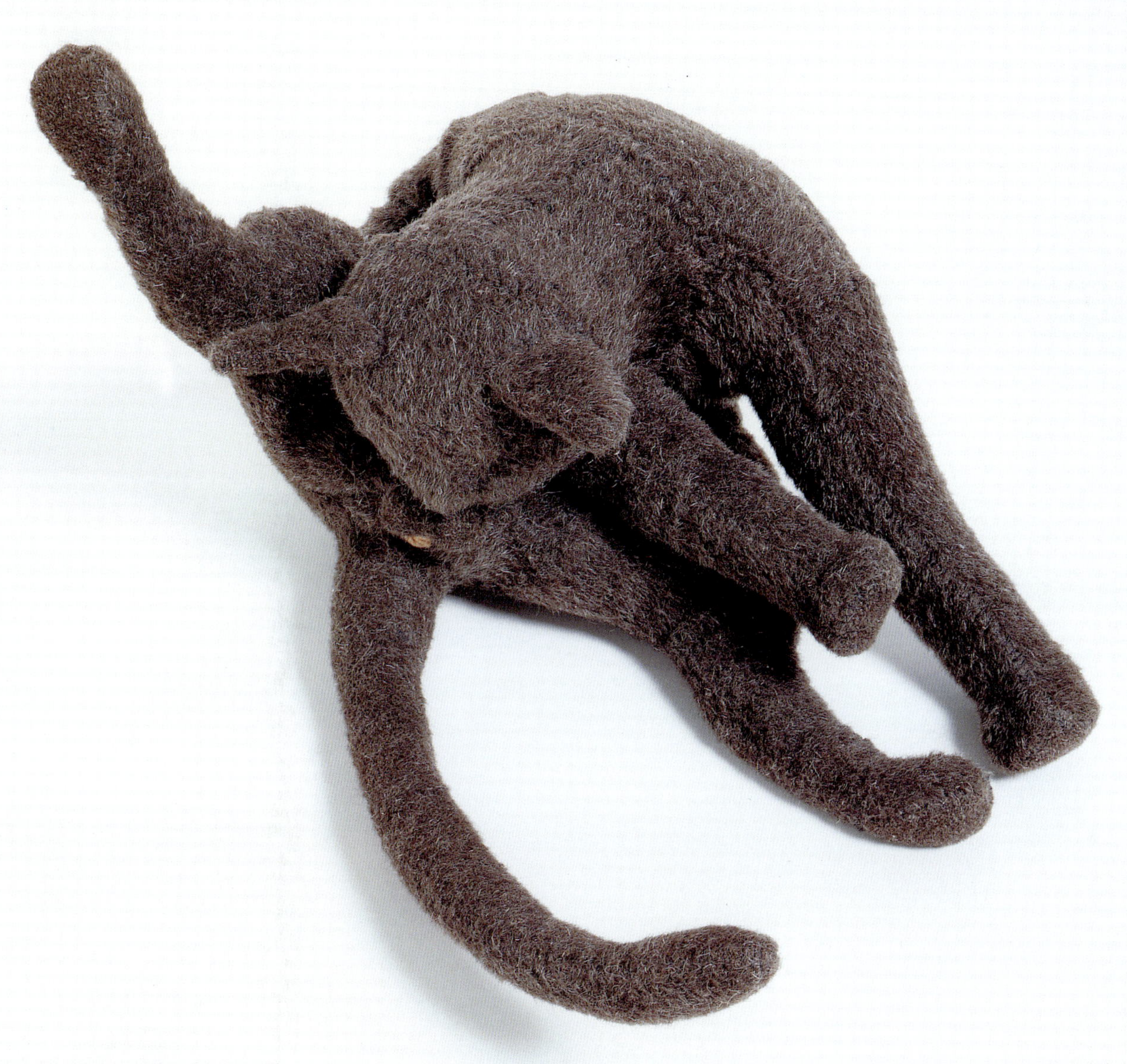

Untitled/Mattress, 1993
Fabric, thread, cotton,
stains, burn
2 x 11 x 15½ inches
Private Collection, London
Photo: Jean Brasilla/
Villa Arson

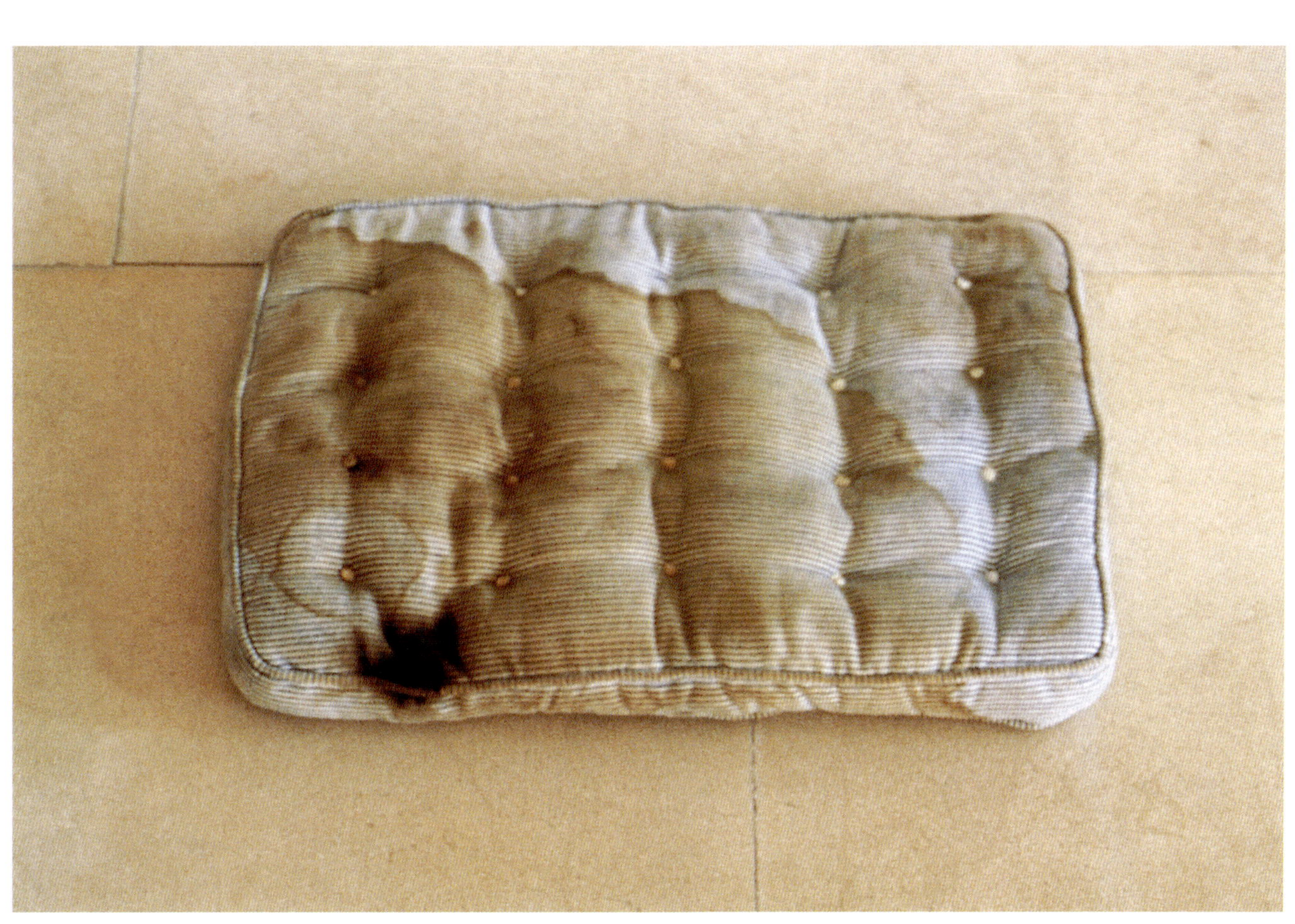

Box for Sewing, 1993
Wood, fabric, thread, card-
board, embroidery floss, paint
40 ½ x 19 ¼ x 17 ¼ inches
Collection: Robert J. Shiffler
Foundation, Greenville, Ohio
Photo: Beth Wessen

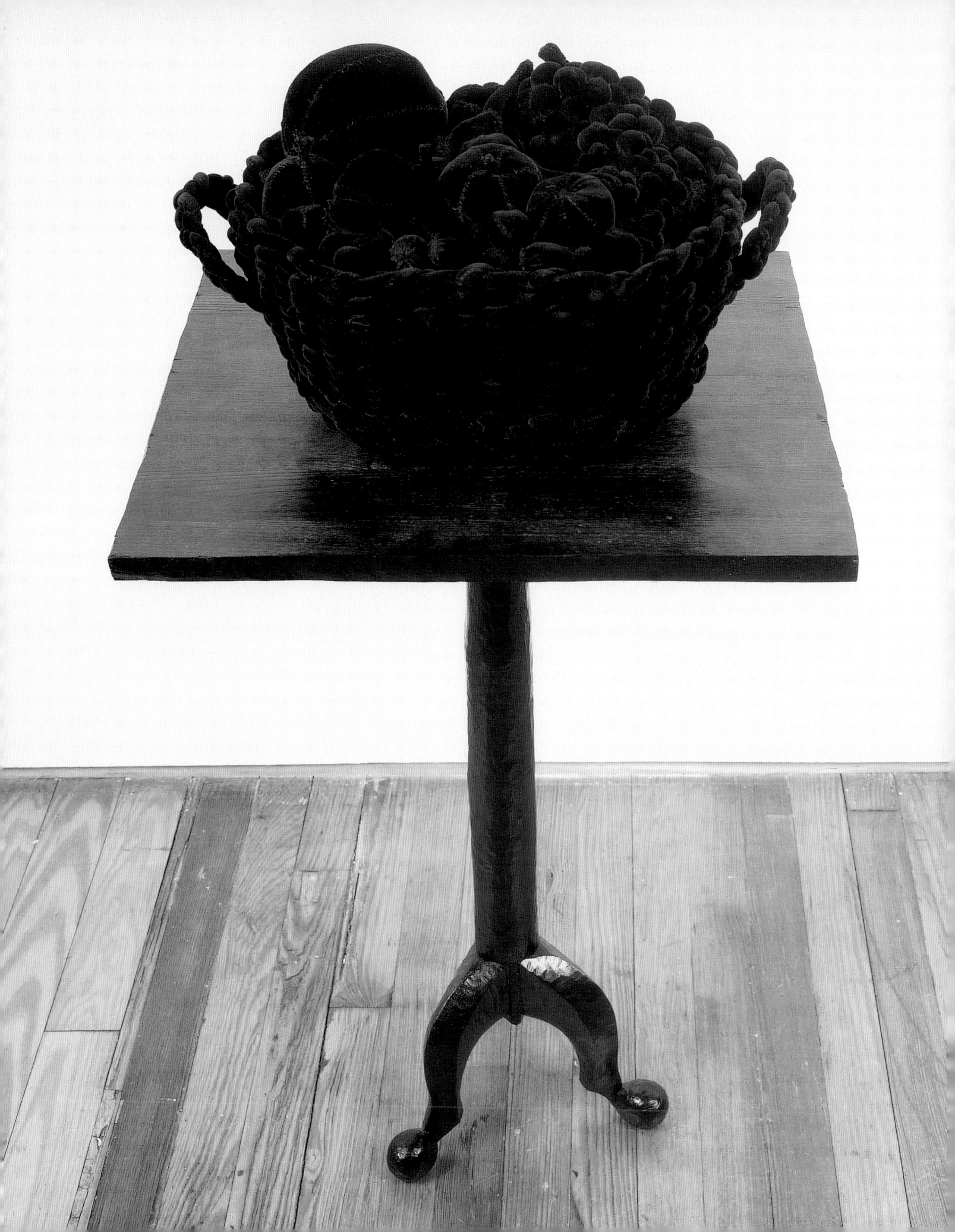

World's Greatest Dad, 1993
Fabric, silkscreen ink,
embroidery floss, wire, etc.
17 x 12 ½ x 6 inches
Collection of Robert J. Shiffler
Foundation, Greenville, Ohio
Photo: Beth Wessen

FOLLOWING PAGE:
Village People, 1995
Mixed media
Approx. 5 inches high x
18 feet long x 4 inches deep
(the work is installed at
9 feet above the floor)
Private Collection, New York

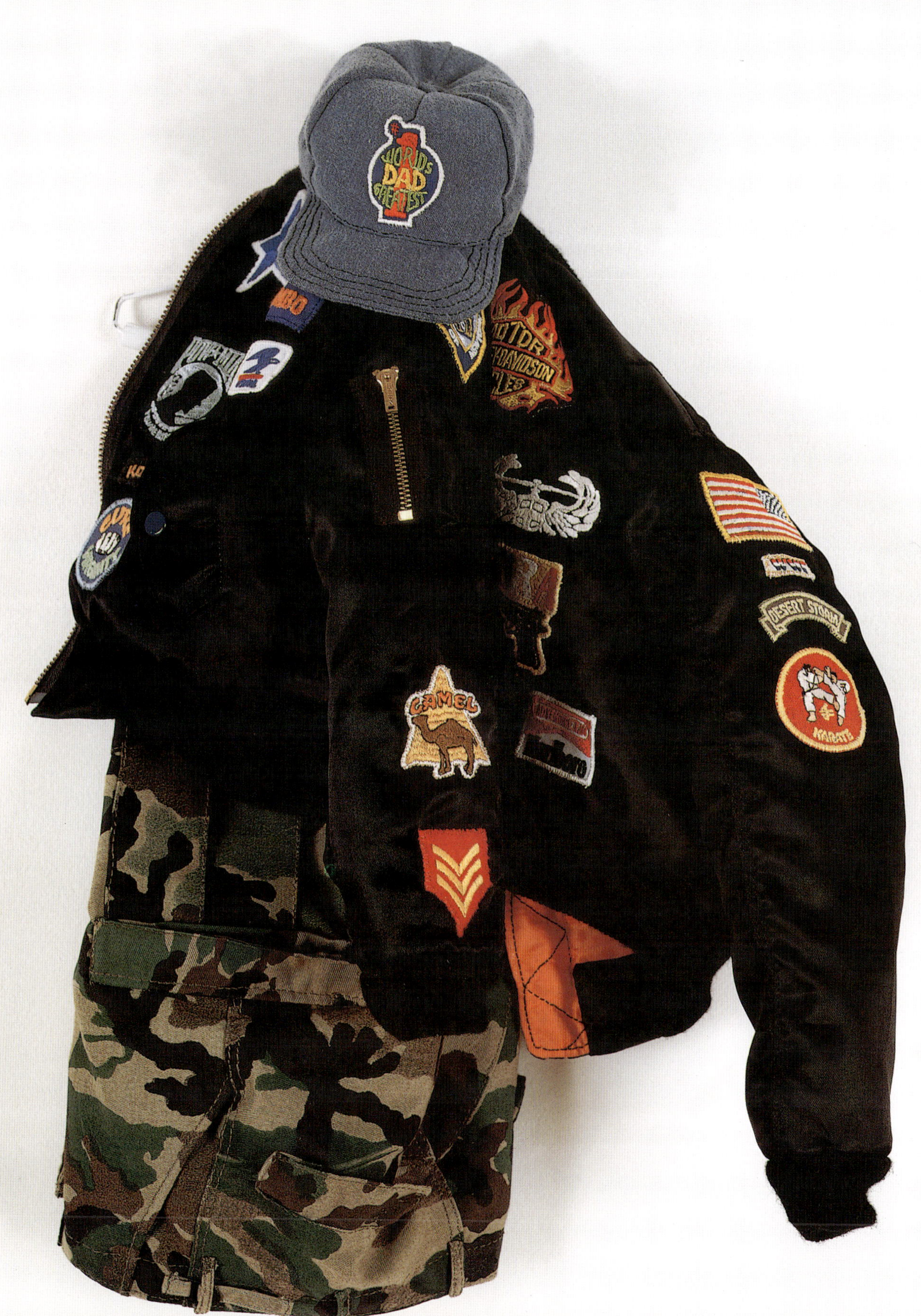
WORLDS DAD GREATEST
CAMEL
DESERT STORM
KARATE

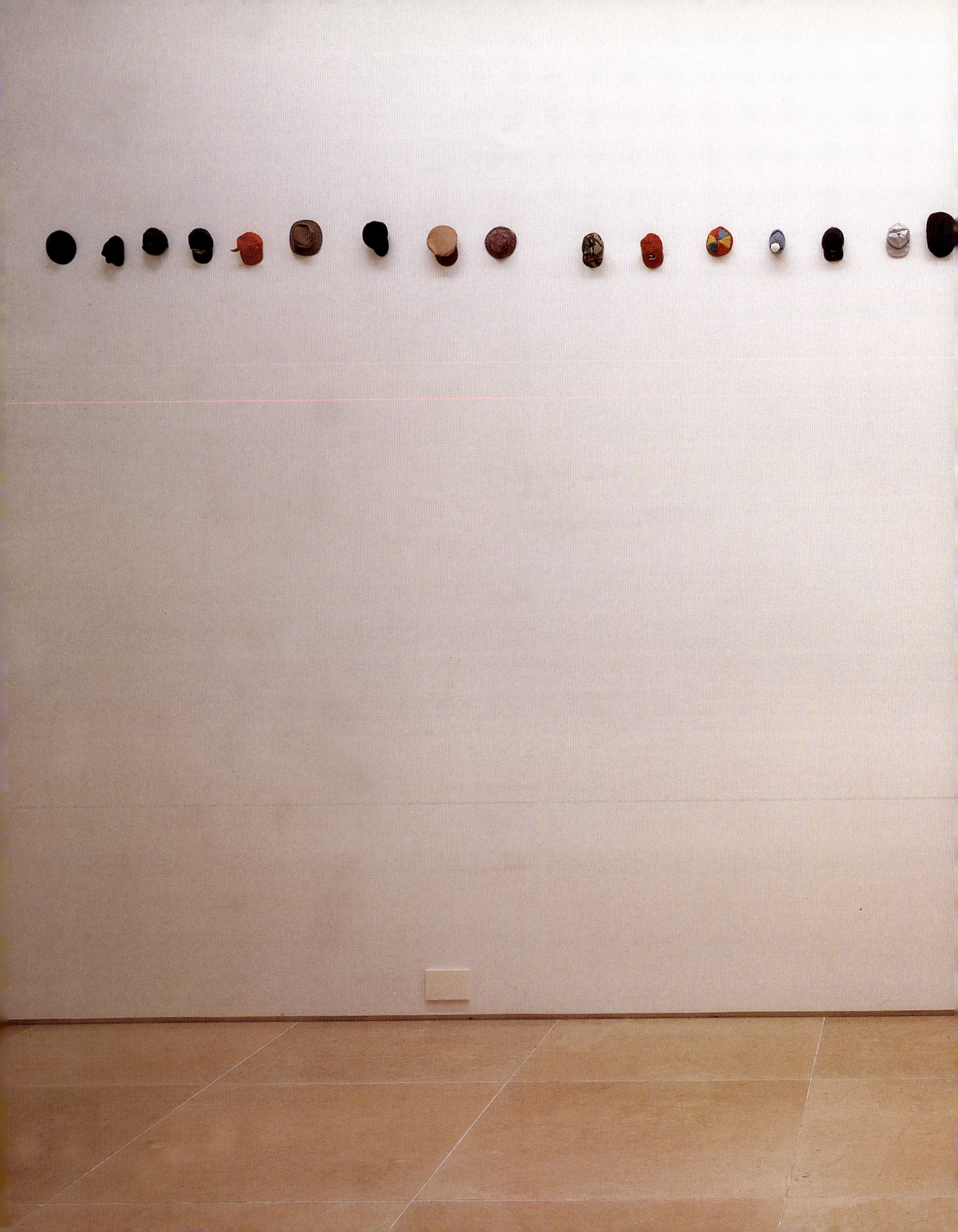

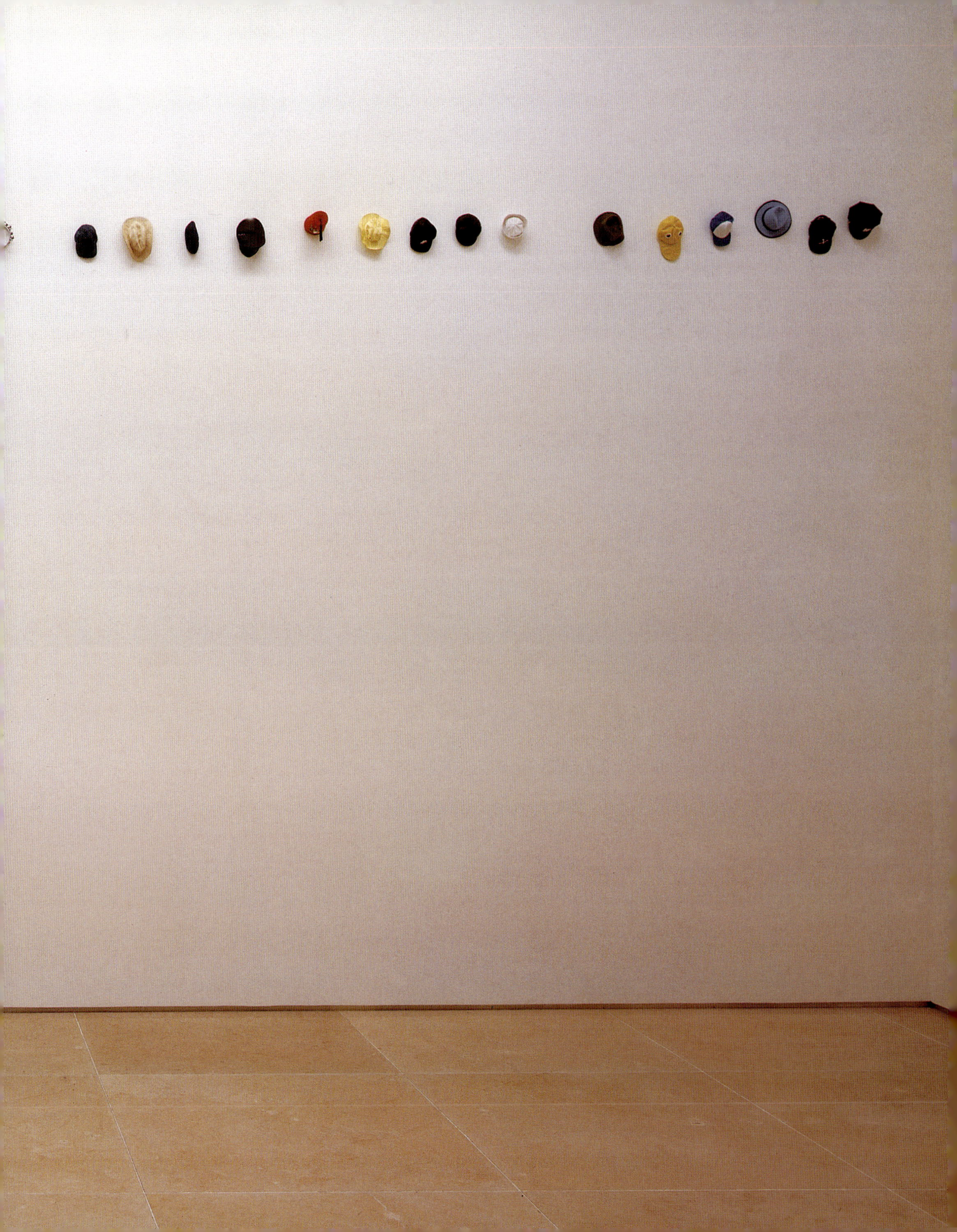

Milk and Honey, 1994–96
2000 hand-thrown porcelain vessels, wood, glass
77 x 30 x 30 inches overall
Whitney Museum of American Art, New York; Purchase, with funds from the Contemporary Painting and Sculpture Committee
Photo: Oren Slor

FOLLOWING PAGE:
Detail, *Milk and Honey*, 1994–96

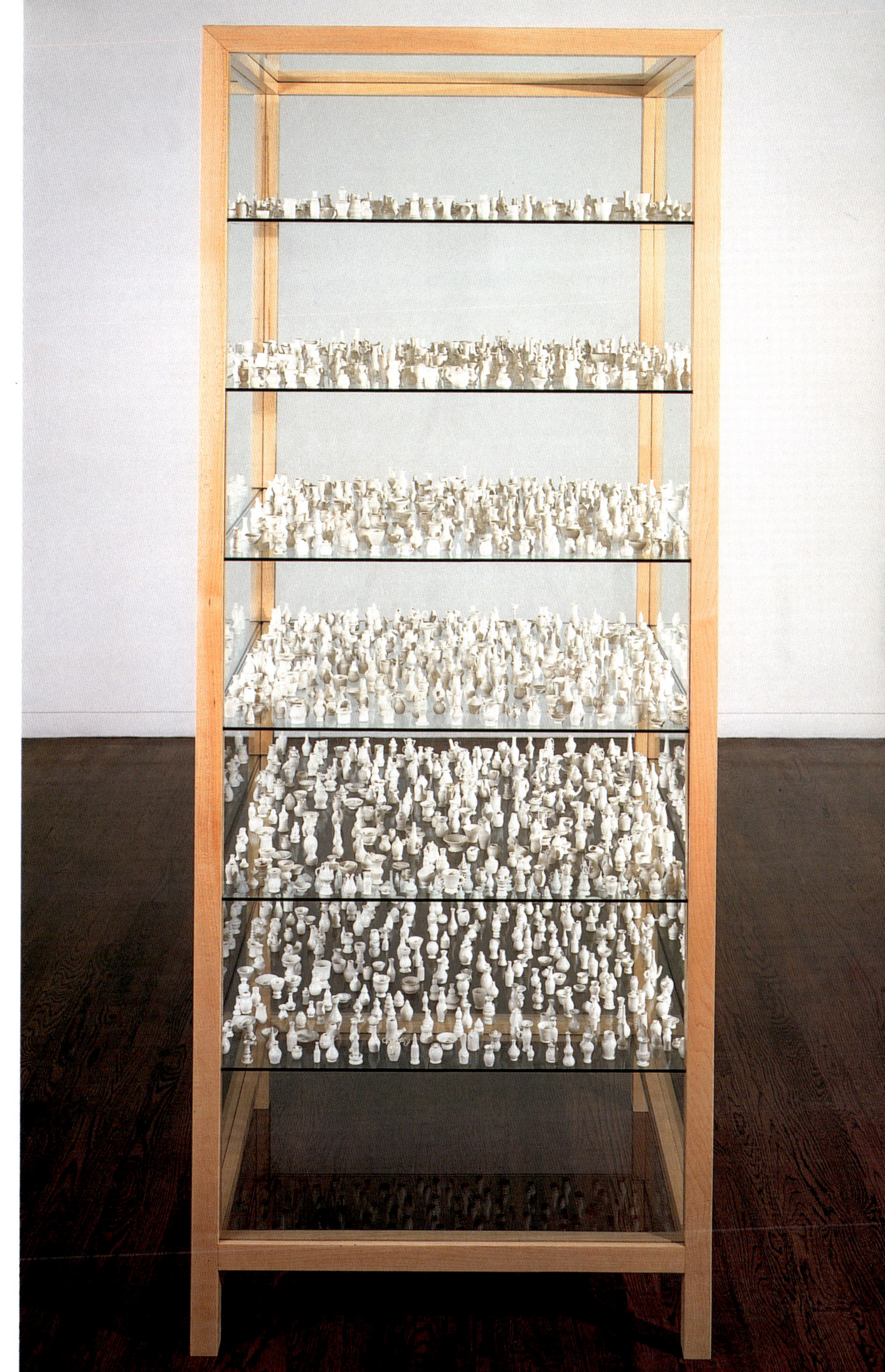

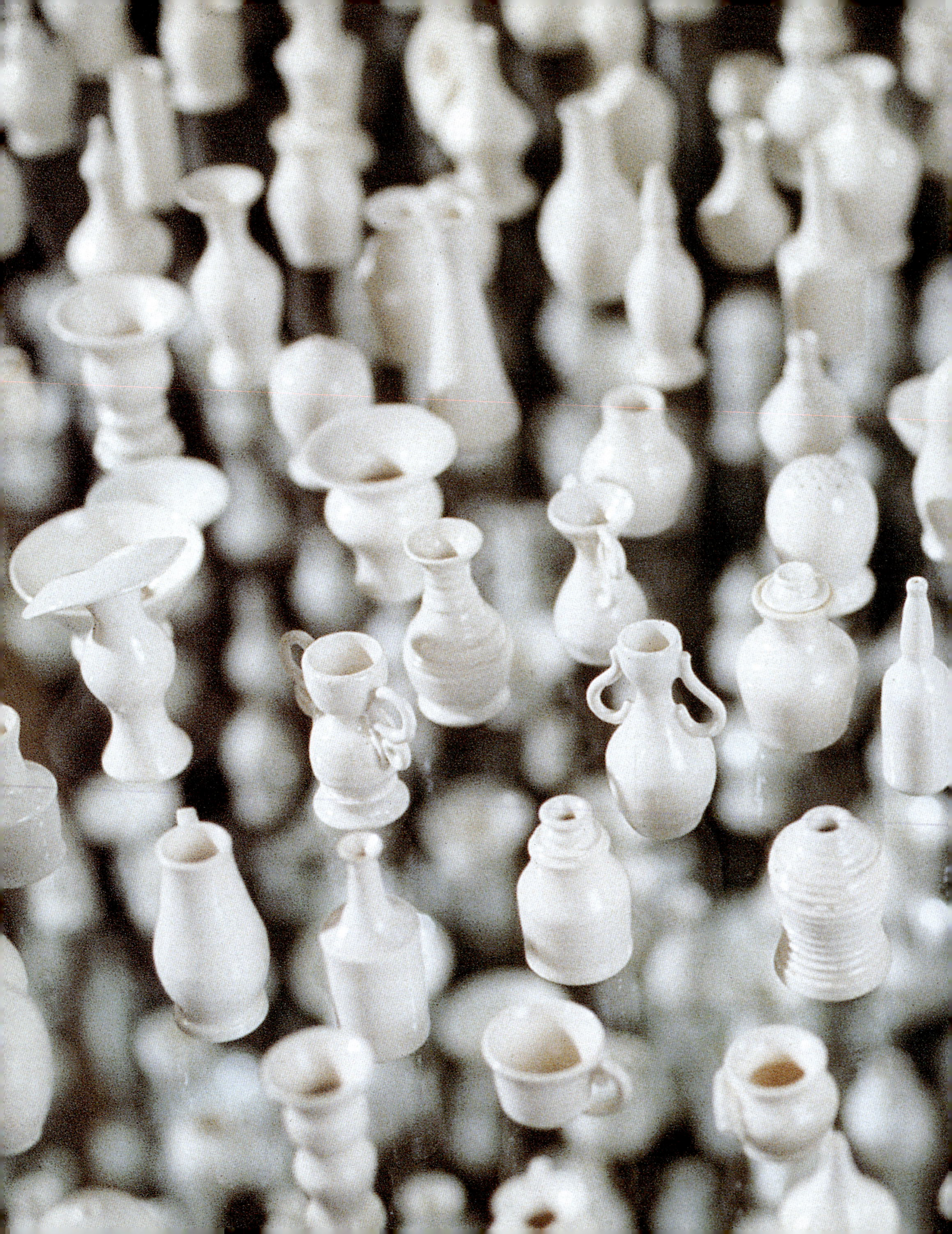

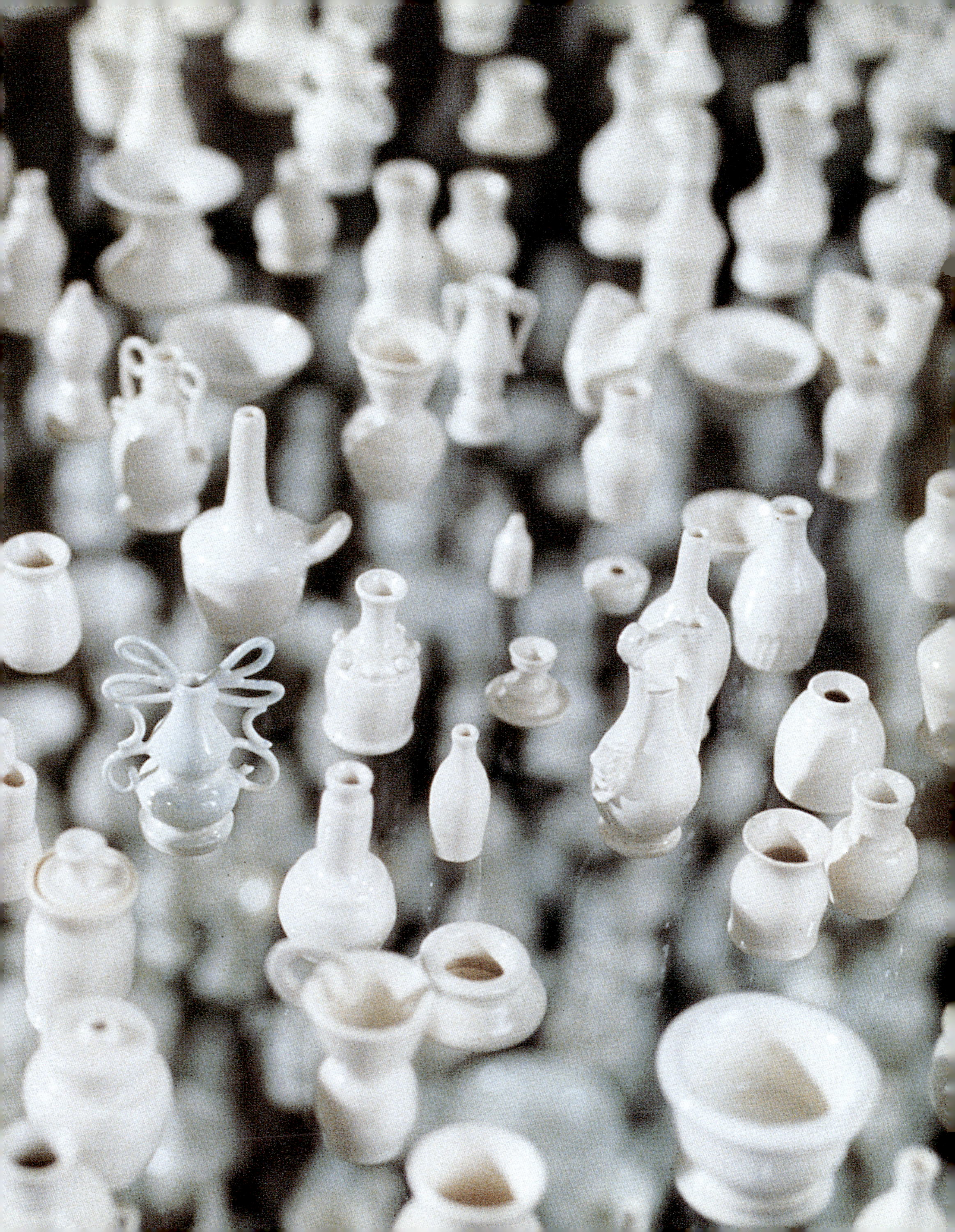

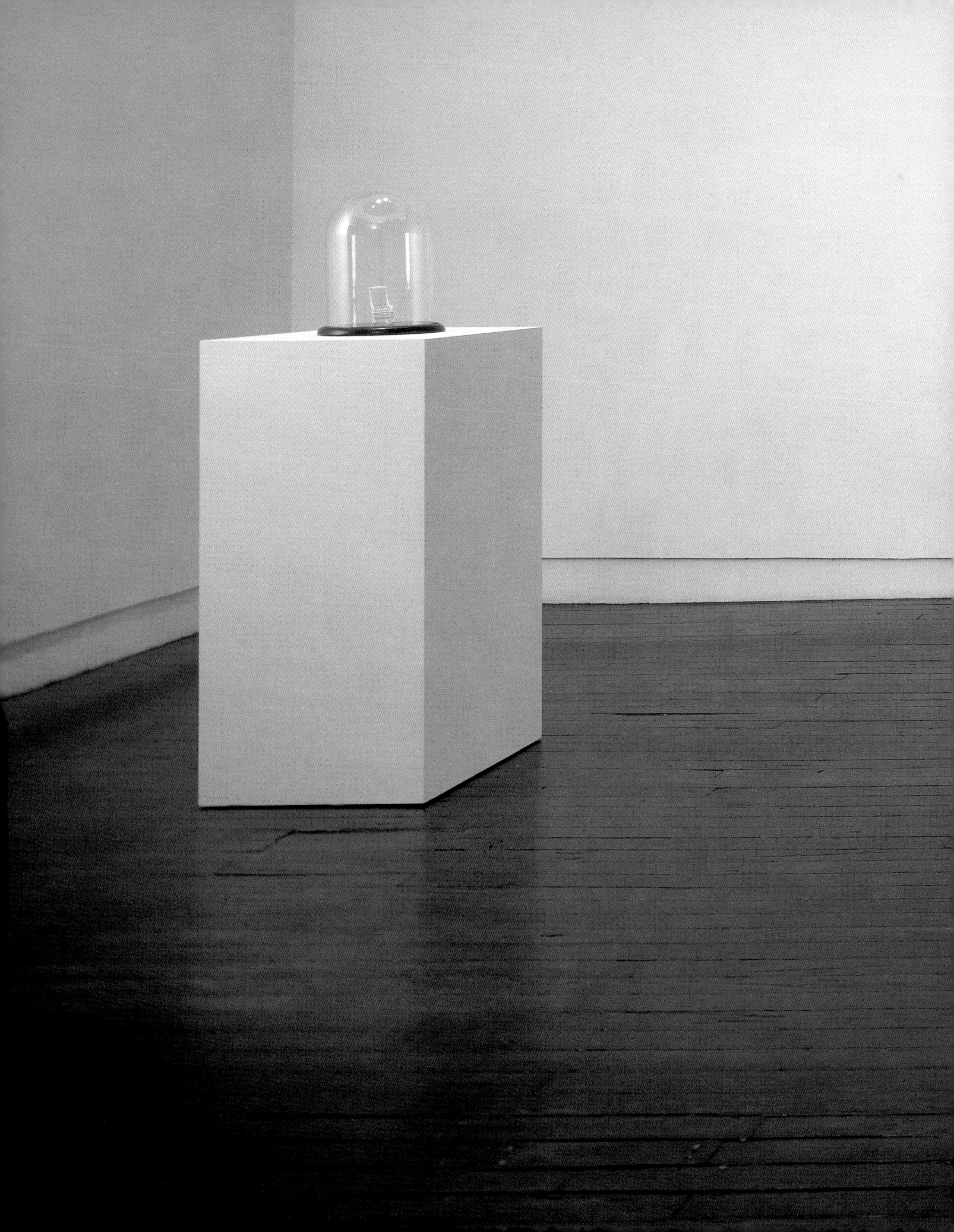

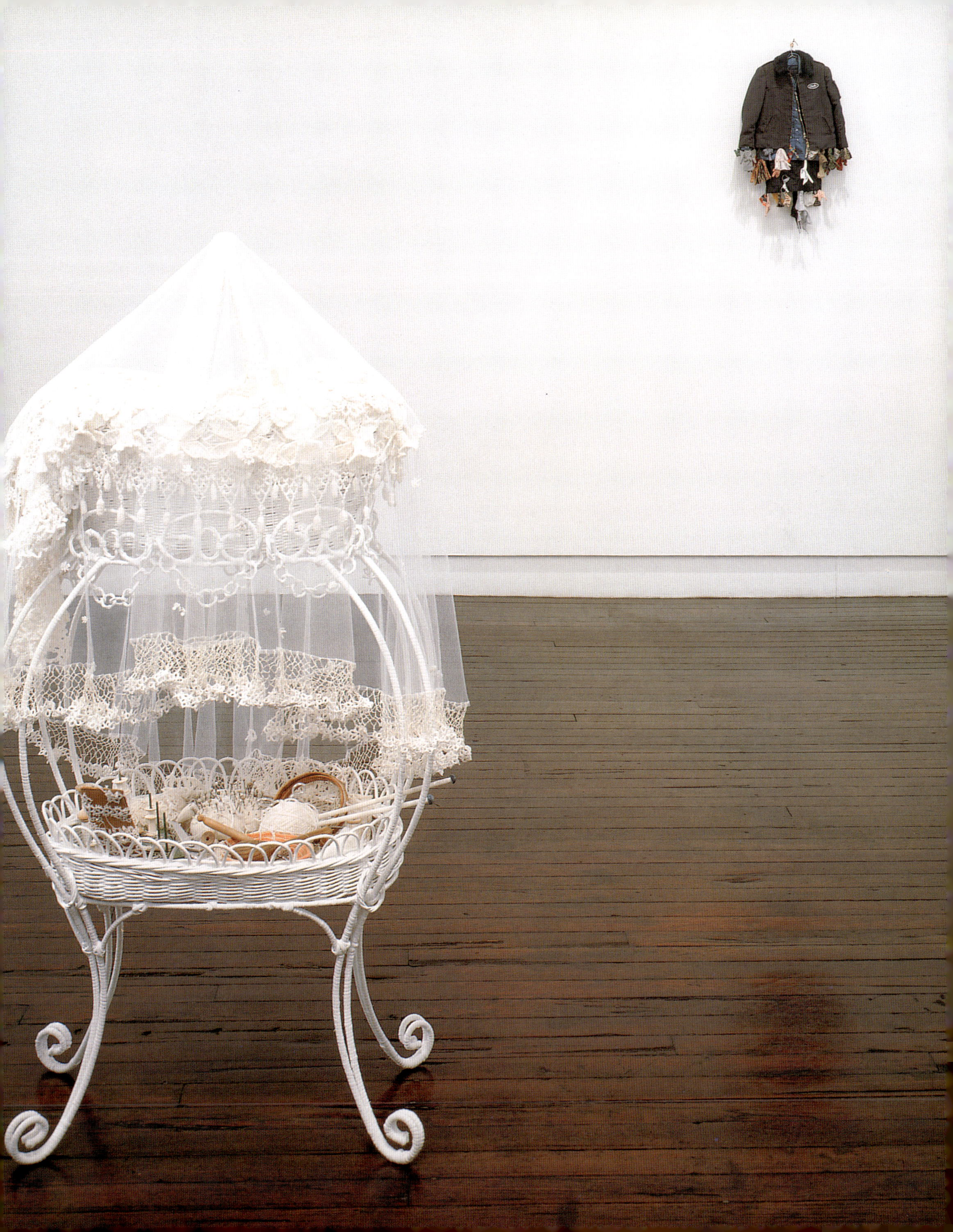

PREVIOUS PAGE:
Installation view, "Charles LeDray," Jay Gorney Modern Art, New York, April 6–May 11, 1996. *Bone Rocker*, 1995; *My Baby*, 1993–96, Mixed media 44½ x 27 x 22 inches Collection Marc and Livia Straus; *Charles*, 1995 Photo: Oren Slor

Pride Flag, 1996
Fabric, thread
192 x 27 x 1 inch
Collection: Eileen and Peter Norton, Santa Monica

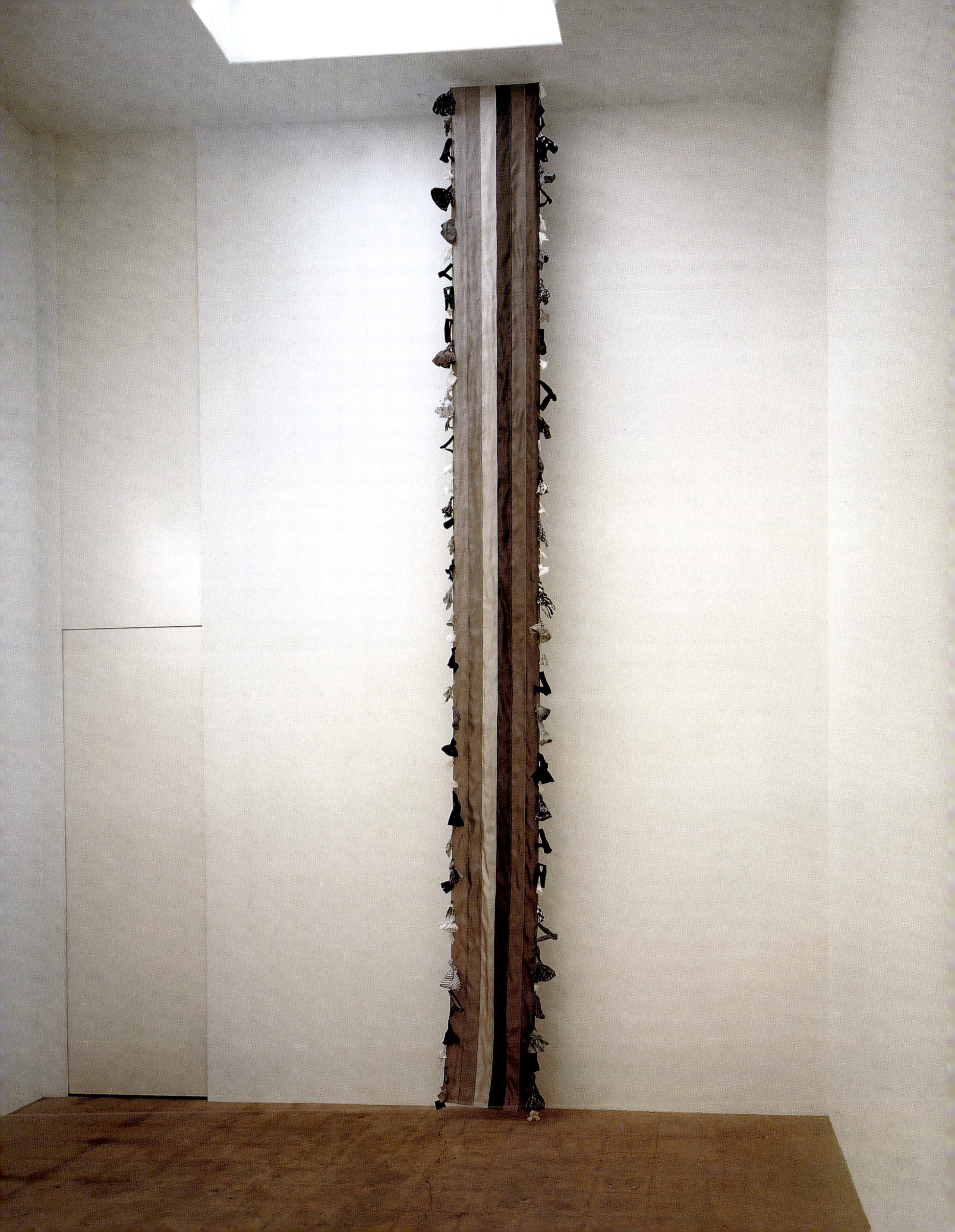

White Tails, 1996
Fabric, thread, wood,
metal, paint, clay
28½ x 10½ x 4 inches
Collection: Jerry Speyer,
New York
Photo: Oren Slor

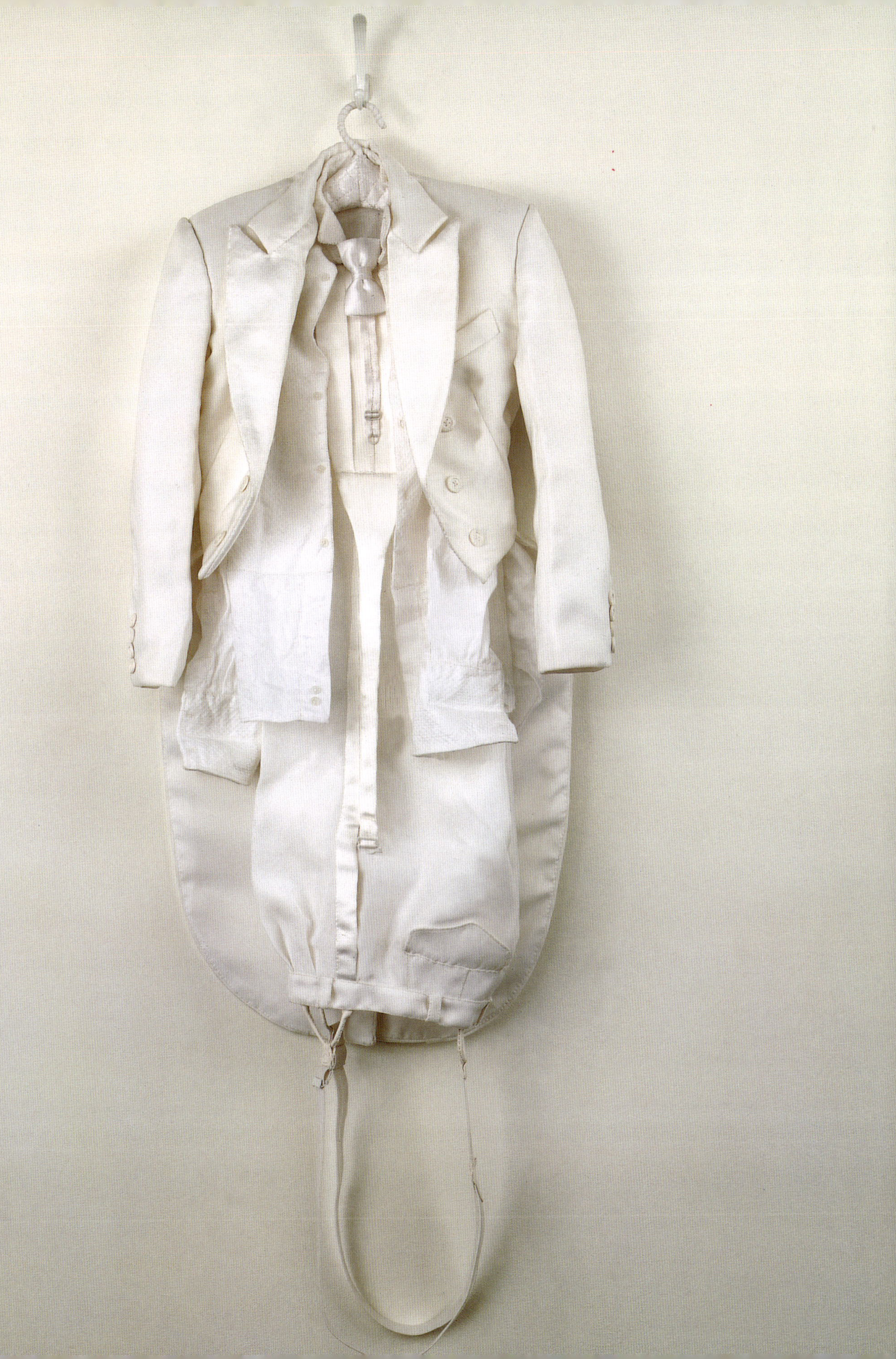

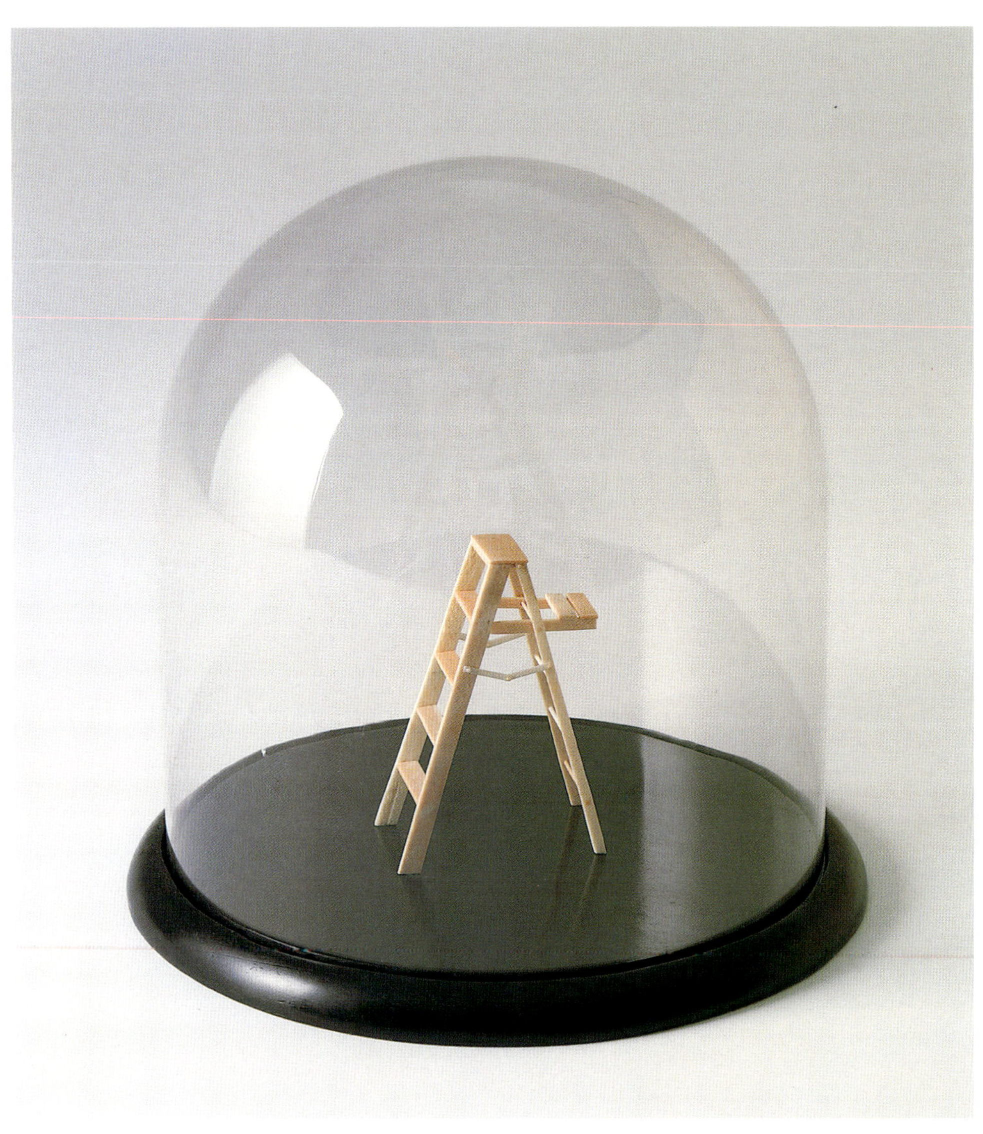

Ladder, 1997, Human bone, glass, wood, 10 ½ x 11 inches overall
Private Collection. Courtesy Sperone Westwater, New York. Photo: D. James Dee

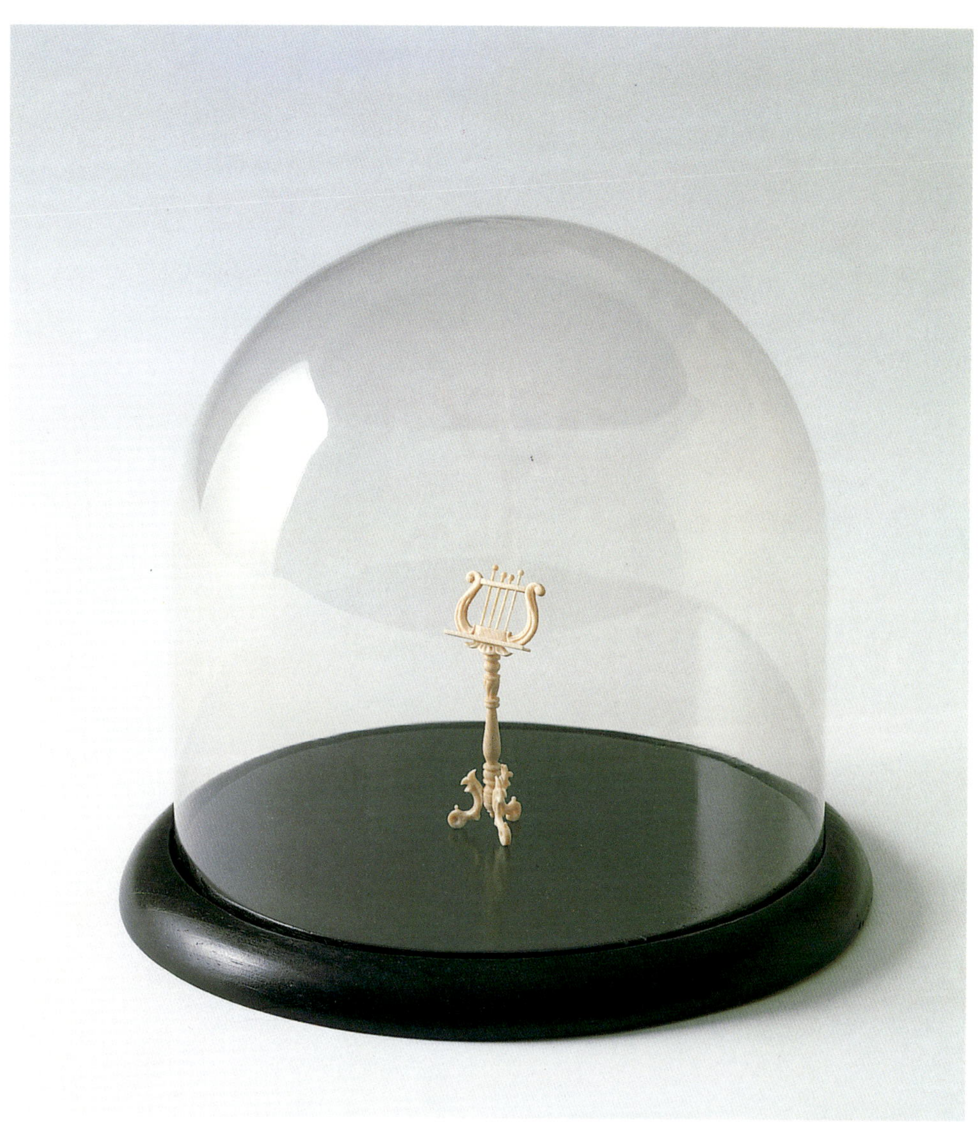

Music Stand, 1997, Human bone, glass, wood, 9⅝ x 8¼ inches overall
Collection: Marianne Boesky, New York, Photo: D. James Dee

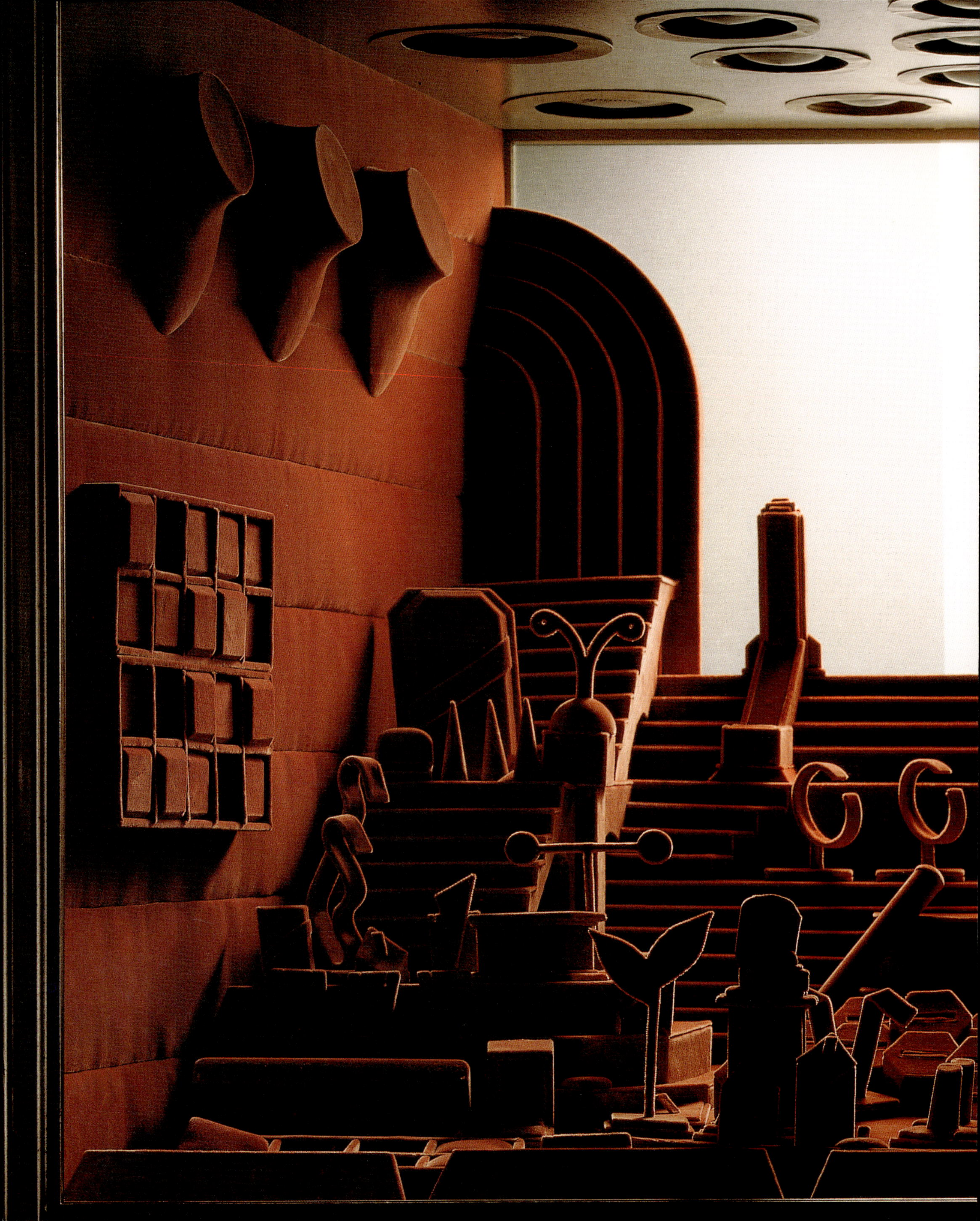

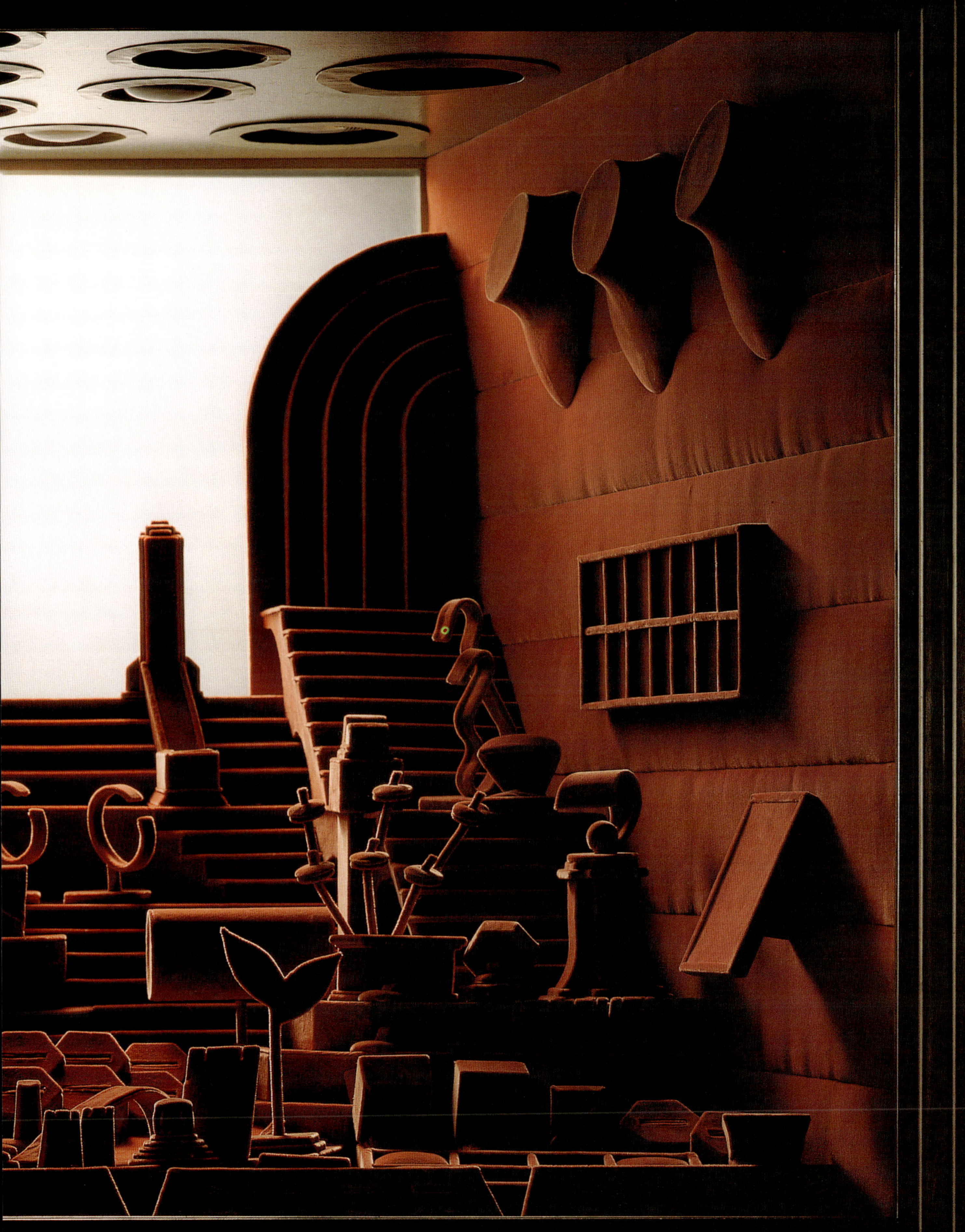

PREVIOUS PAGE:
Jewelry Display Window, 1998
Fabric, metal, plastic, paint, glass, cardboard, electric lights
40 x 44 x 22 inches
Collection of Des Moines Art Center, Des Moines, Iowa
Photo: Guy L'Heureux

Bust, 1995
Fabric, thread, plastic, paint, metal, wood
7 x 12 x 4 inches
Collection of Nancy and Joel Portnoy, New York
Photo: Oren Slor

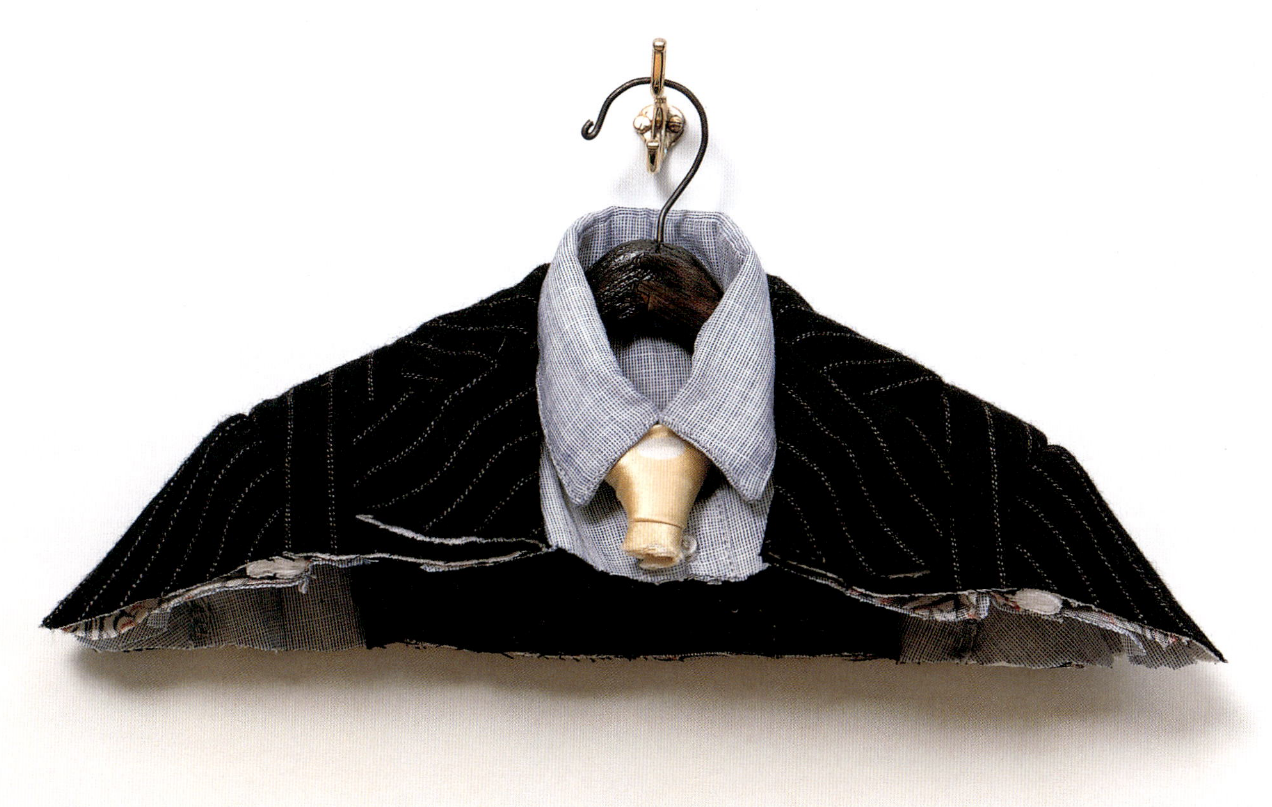

Chuck, 1997
Fabric, metal, plastic, thread
29 x 11[illegible] x 6[illegible] inches
The Frank Cohen Collection,
England
Photo: Oren Slor

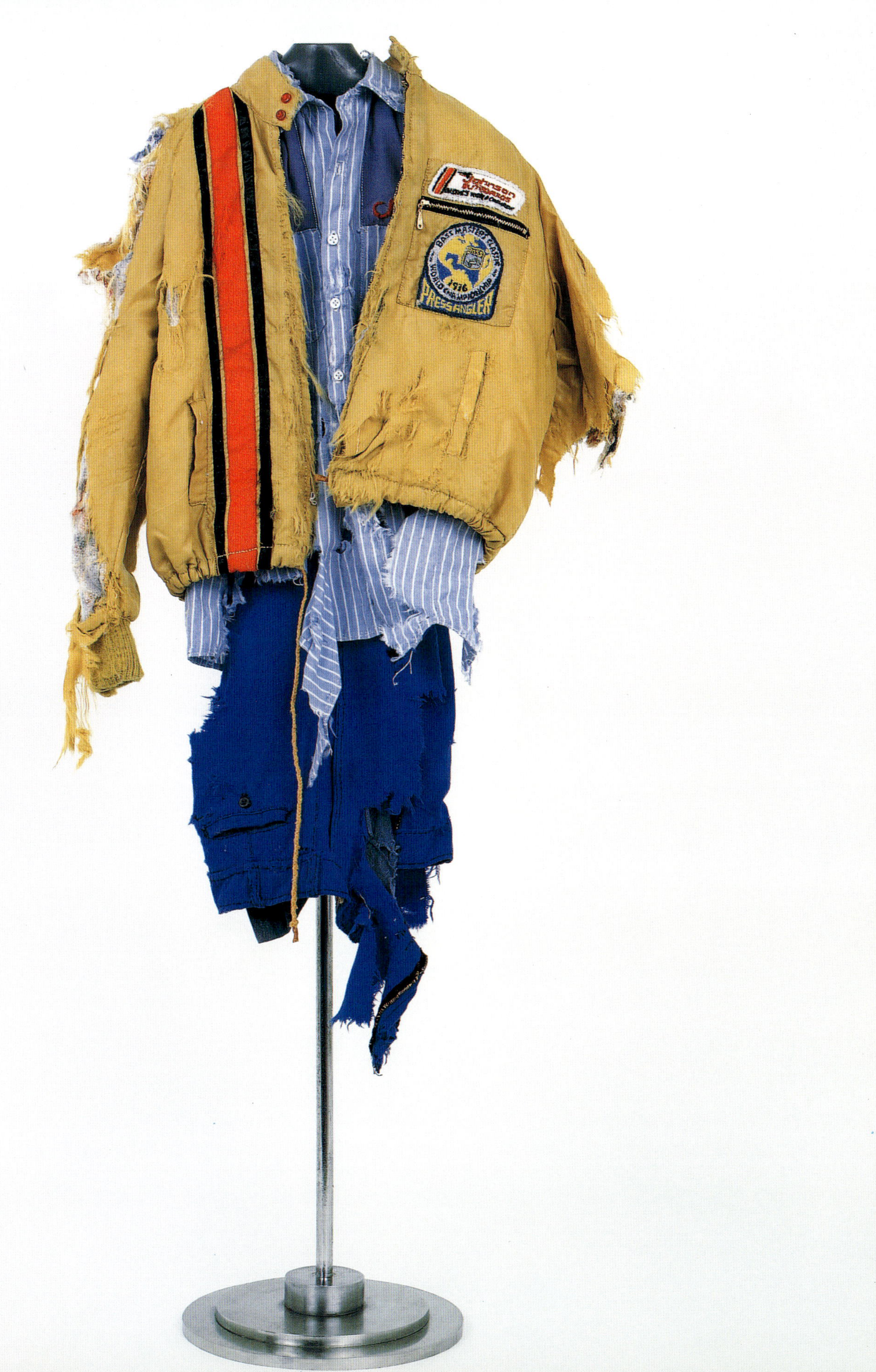
Johnson
BASS MASTERS CLASSIC
WORLD CHAMPIONSHIP
1976
PRESS ANGLER

Torn Suit, 1997–98
Fabric, thread, wood,
metal, plastic,
animal horn, acrylic paint
29¼ x 13 x 3[illegible] inches
Collection: Eileen and
Peter Norton,
Santa Monica, California
Photo: Oren Slor

FOLLOWING PAGE:
Wheat, 2000
Human bone
[illegible] x 24 x 6[illegible] inches
Courtesy of the artist
and Sperone Westwater,
New York
Photo: Oren Slor

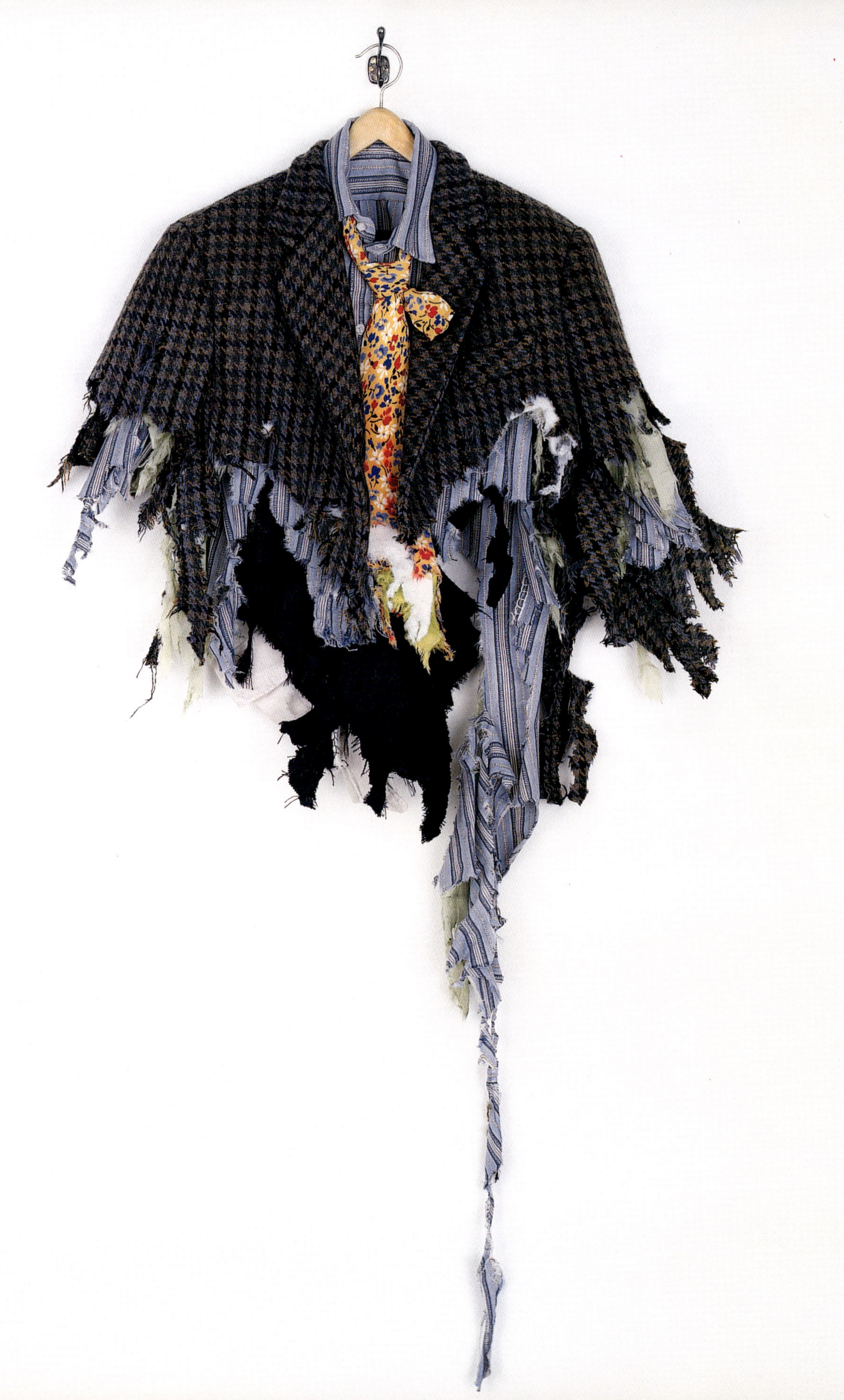

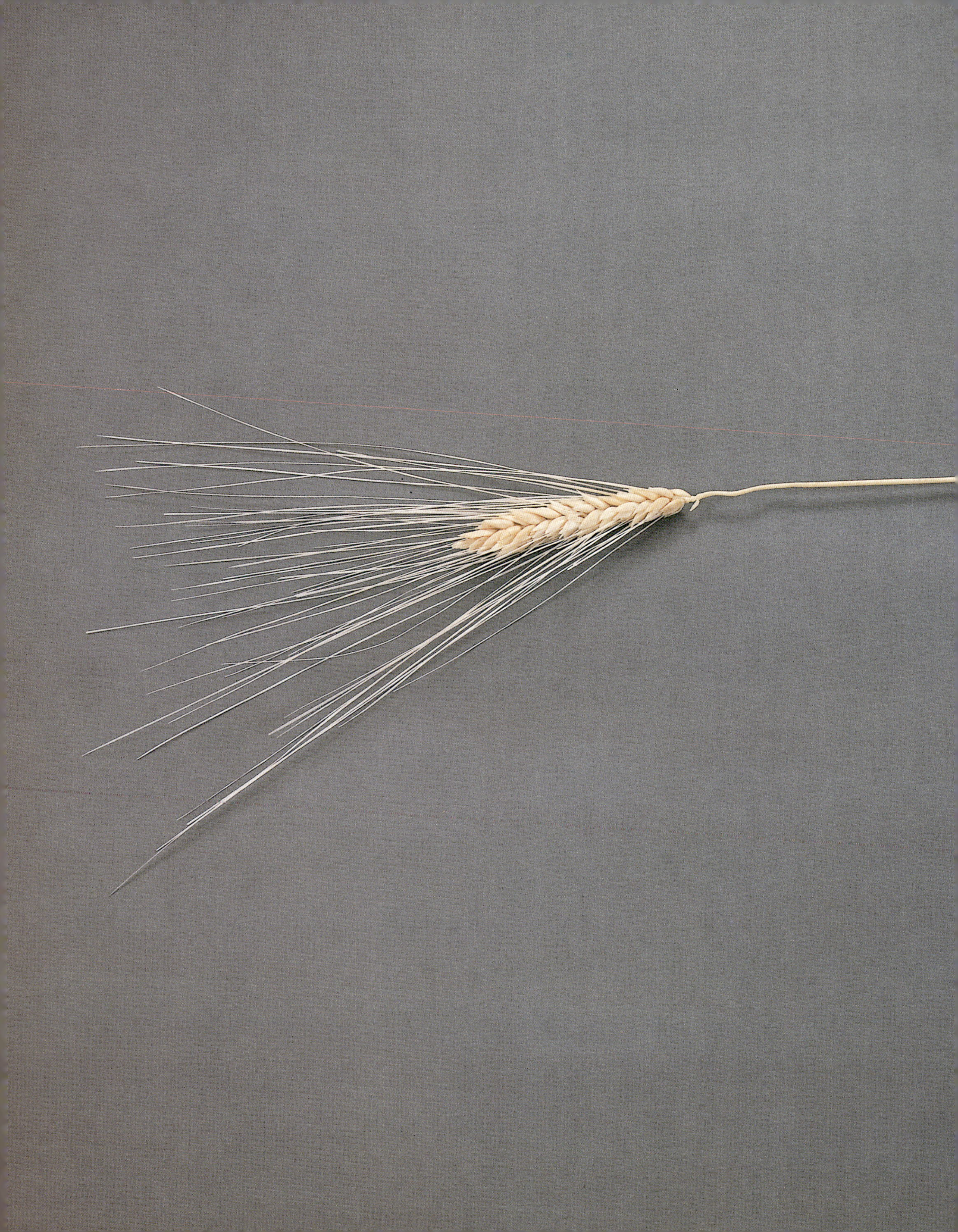

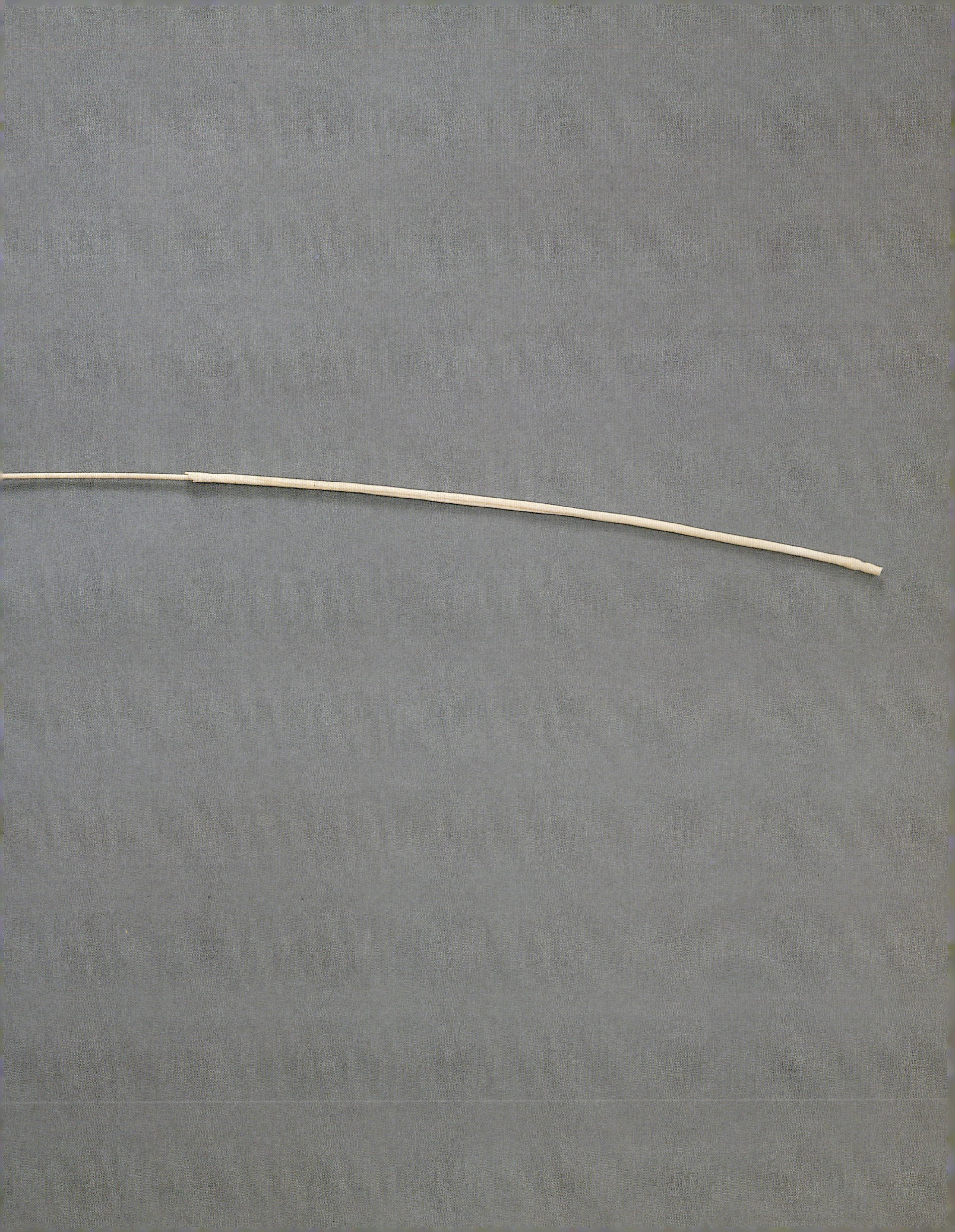

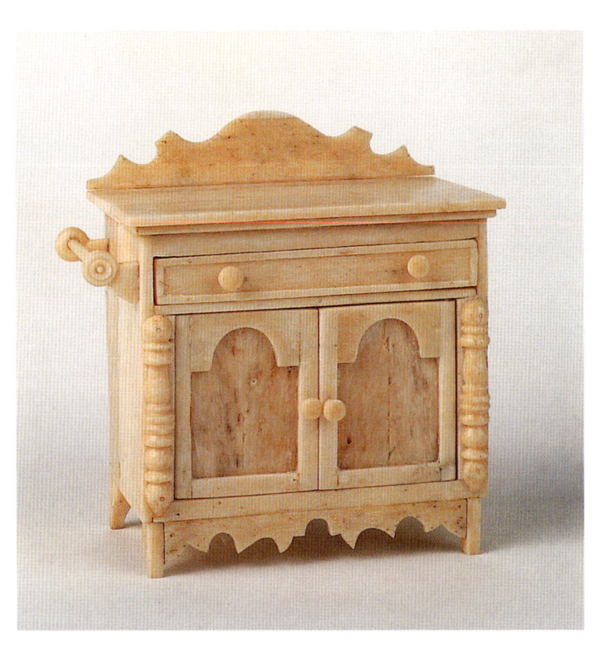

Washstand, 1999, Human bone, 2 ⅜ x 2 5/16 x 1 ¼ inches, Private Collection, Courtesy Sperone Westwater, New York, Photo: Oren Slor

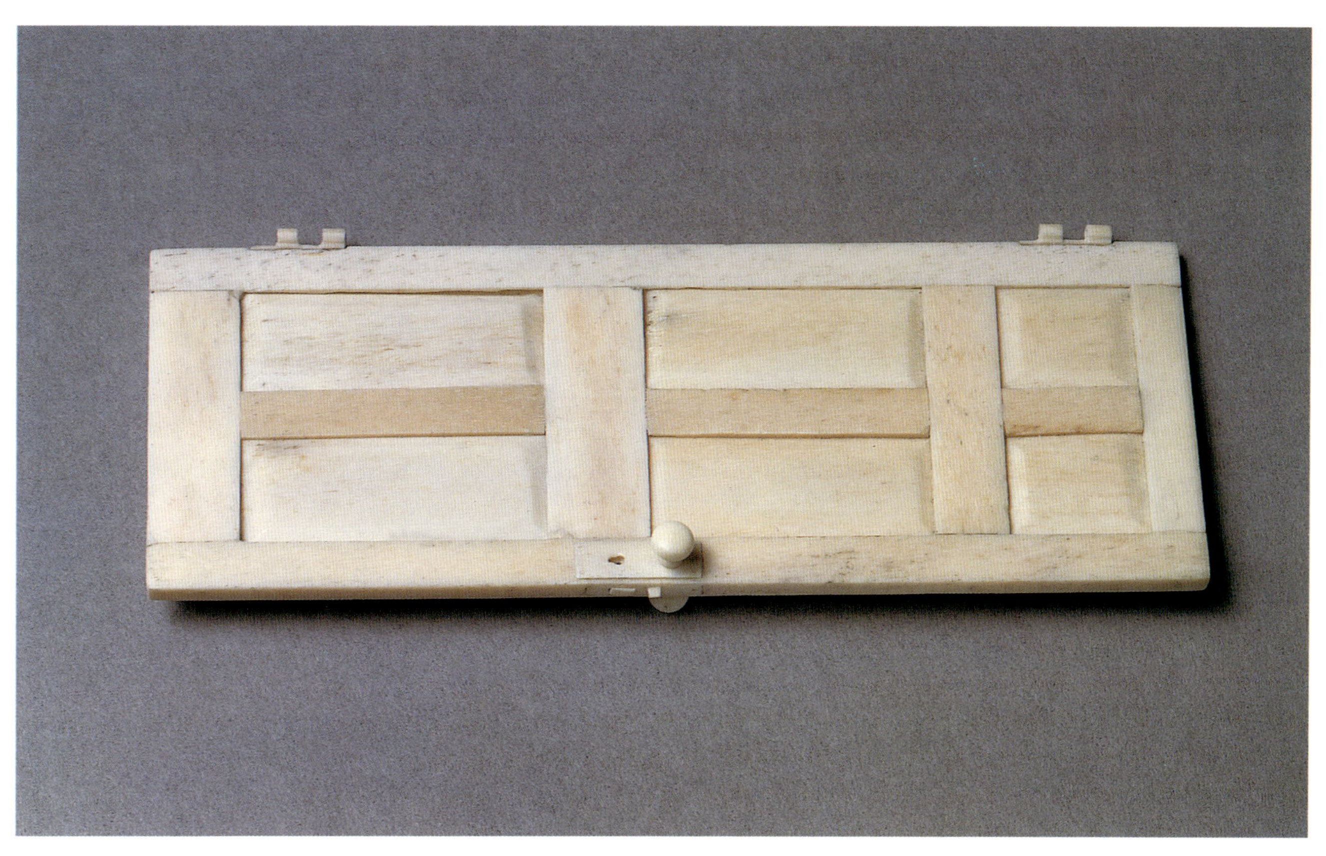

Door, 1999, Human bone, ⅜ x 5¼ x 2 inches, Private Collection, New York, Photo: D. James Dee

Untitled/Tower, 1999–2000
Human bone
18 [illegible] x 9 x 4 [illegible] inches
Collection: The
Wadsworth Atheneum,
Hartford, Connecticut,
gift of Janice and
Mickey Cartin
Photo: D. James Dee

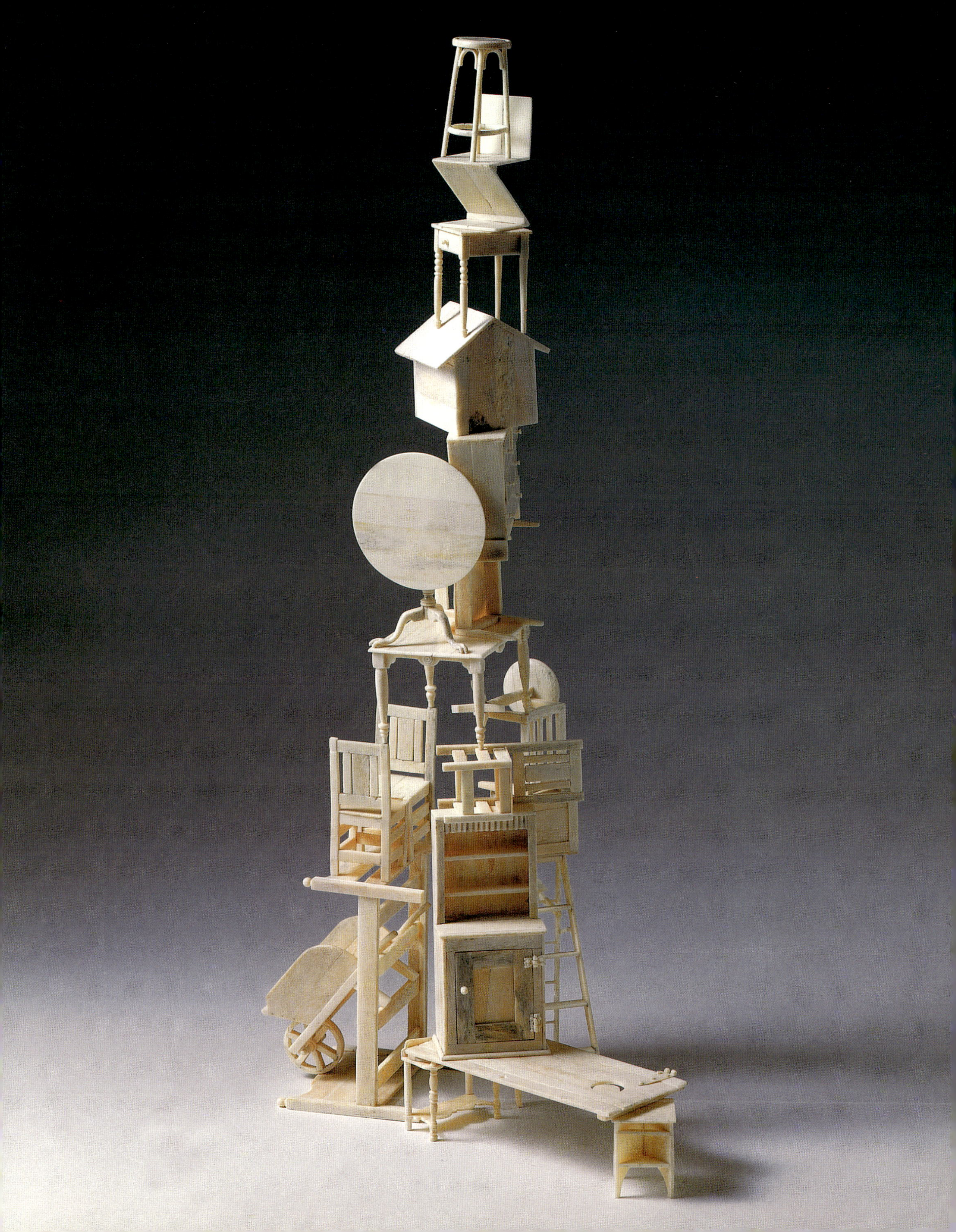

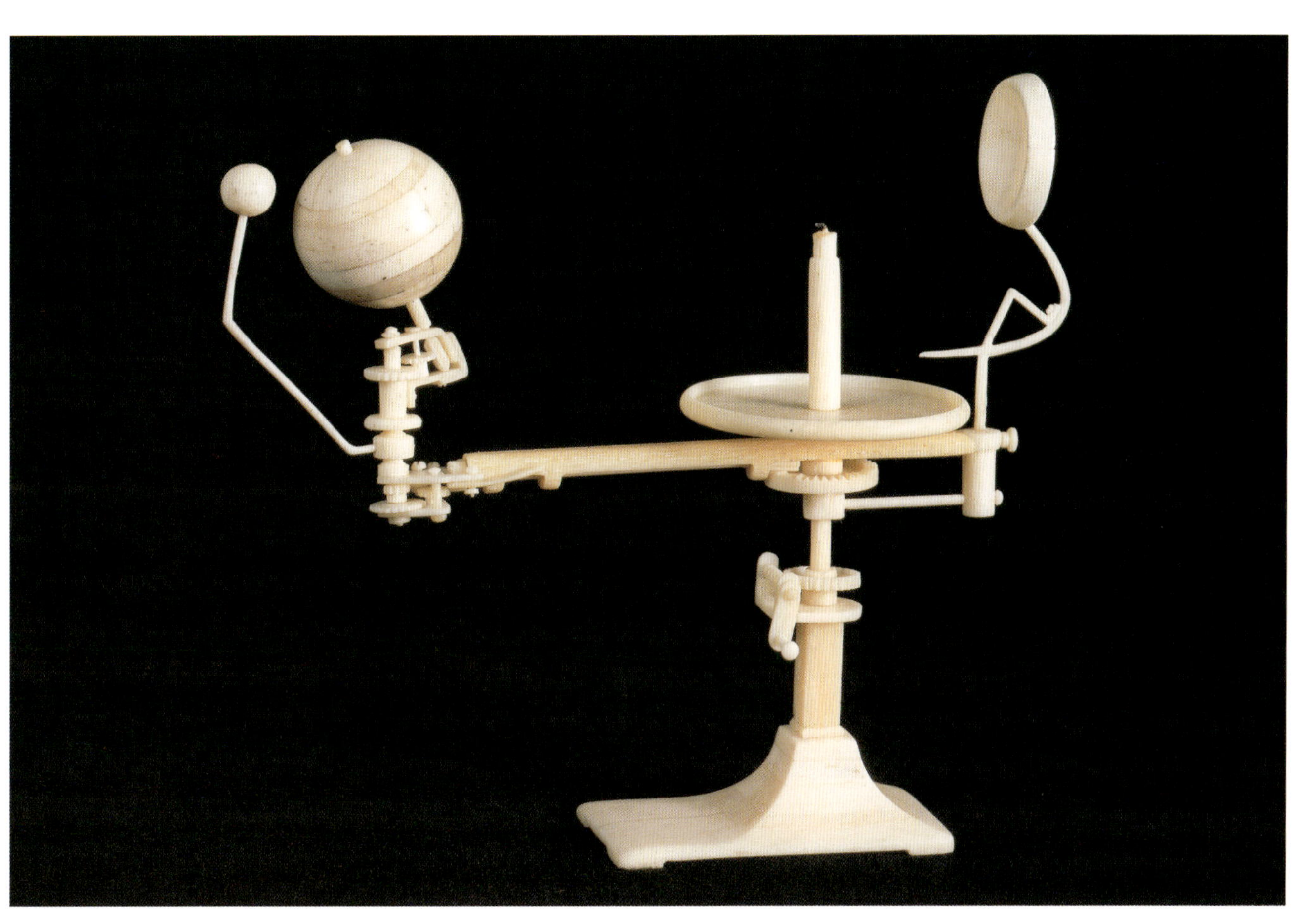

Tellurian, 2000. Human bone, 3¼ x 3⅞ x 1¼ inches.
Courtesy of the artist and Sperone Westwater, New York. Photo: Oren Slor

Works in the Exhibition

Mourning Piece, 1989. Fabric, thread, wood, glass, buttons, paper tape 9 ¾ x 19 ½ inches. The Carol and Arthur Goldberg Collection, New York

Untitled (Bear in a corset box), 1989. Velvet, buttons, wood, paper, fabric, nails, brassiere box. 11 ¼ x 5 ¾ x 3 ¼ inches. Private Collection, New York

King of the Road, 1991. Underwear, found quilt, buttons. 74 ½ x 54 ½ inches Collection of Walter Sudol and Steven Johnson, New York

My Hands, My Father's Hands, #2, 1991. Cotton, wood, thread, mother of pearl, paper tape, glass. 12 x 9 inches. Collection of Ruth & Jake Bloom, Marina del Rey, California

Untitled (Tar bear), 1991. Tar, velvet, buttons, thread, sawdust, sugar, porcelain 14 ½ x 20 x 4 inches. Collection of Ralph Balass, New York

** *workworkworkworkwork*, 1991. 588 mixed-media objects. Approx. 45 feet long x 10 inches wide x 2 inches deep. Collection of Robert J. Shiffler Foundation, Greenville, Ohio

Becoming/Mister Man, 1992. Fabric, thread, wire. 14 x 12 ½ x 4 ½ inches Private Collection, New York

Untitled (Bear with one leg), 1992. Velvet, cotton, thread, wire. 11 x 5 x 4 inches Private Collection

Collecting Teeth, 1993. Porcelain, fabric, thread. ¼ x 12 x 12 inches. Private Collection. Courtesy Sperone Westwater, New York

Pretty Teacher, 1993. Fabric, wire, thread, cotton. 15 ¾ x 12 ½ x 8 ¼ inches Private Collection. Courtesy of Sperone Westwater, New York

Untitled (Broken bear), 1993. Leather, cotton, thread. 5 ¼ x 3 ¾ x 1 ½ inches Collection of Kenneth L. Freed, Boston

Untitled/Clothesline, 1993. Fabric, thread, buttons. 34 feet x 3½ inches x 5 inches Collection of Susan and Michael Hort, New York

Untitled/Mattress, 1993. Fabric, thread, cotton, stains, burn. 2 x 11 x 15½ inches Private Collection, London

Village People, 1993. Mixed media. Approx. 5 inches high x 18 feet long x 4 inches deep. (the work is installed at 9 feet above the floor) Private Collection, New York

*** *World's Greatest Dad*, 1993. Fabric, silkscreen ink, embroidery floss, wire, etc. 17 x 12½ x 6 inches. Collection of Robert J. Shiffler Foundation, Greenville, Ohio

S.A.M., 1994. Fabric, thread, metal, plastic, paint. 25¾ x 11 x 4 inches Courtesy of Merrill Wright, Seattle, Washington

*** *Village People*, 1994. Mixed media. Approx. 5 inches high x 19 feet long x 4 inches deep. (the work is installed at 9 feet above the floor) Private collection, New York

Milk and Honey, 1994–96. 2000 hand-thrown porcelain vessels, wood, glass 77 x 30 x 30 inches overall. Whitney Museum of American Art, New York; Purchase, with funds from the Contemporary Painting and Sculpture Committee

Bust, 1995. Fabric, thread, plastic, paint, metal, wood. 7 x 12 x 4 inches Collection of Nancy and Joel Portnoy, New York

Charles, 1995. Fabric, thread, metal, plastic, paint. 19 x 14 x 4½ inches Collection of Barbara and Leonard Kaban, Charlestown, Massachusetts

Come Together, 1995–96. Fabric, thread, embroidery floss, metal. 34½ x 26 x 6½ inches. Collection San Francisco Museum of Modern Art, San Francisco. Purchased through a gift of Kimberly S. L. Knight and John B. Knight III

* *Chuck*, 1997. Fabric, metal, plastic, thread. 29 x 11½ x 6½ inches The Frank Cohen Collection, England

Torn Suit, 1997–98. Fabric, thread, wood, metal, plastic, animal horn, acrylic paint. 29¼ x 13 x 3¼ inches. Collection of Eileen and Peter Norton, Santa Monica, California

Door, 1999. Human bone. ⅛ x 5¼ x 2 inches. Private Collection, New York

Washstand, 1999. Human bone. 2⅜ x 2 5/16 x 1¼ inches. Private Collection. Courtesy Sperone Westwater, New York

Tellurian, 2000. Human bone. 3¼ x 3⅜ x 1¼ inches. Courtesy of the artist and Sperone Westwater, New York

Wheat, 2000. Human bone. ½ x 24 x 6½ inches. Courtesy of the artist and Sperone Westwater, New York

Buttons, 2000–2001. Human bone. 130 buttons, approx. ¼ x 14 x 14 inches Courtesy of the artist and Sperone Westwater, New York

Jewelry Window, 2002. Fabric, thread, wood, metal, glass, plastic, paint, electric light. Approx. 54 x 75 x 42 inches. Courtesy of the artist and Sperone Westwater, New York

Village People, 1997–2002. Mixed media. Approx. 10 inches high x 18 feet wide x 9 inches deep. (the work is installed at 9 feet above the floor) Private Collection. Courtesy Sperone Westwater, New York

*	Showing only at ICA
**	Showing only at ICA and the Seattle Art Museum
***	Showing only at Yerba Buena Center for the Arts and the Seattle Art Museum

Exhibition History

Born: Seattle, Washington, 1960
Lives and works in New York City

Awards and Residencies

1998 Academy Award, American Academy of Arts and Letters.

1997–1998 Gorham Phillips Stevens Visual Arts Fellowship, American Academy in Rome.

1993 The Louis Comfort Tiffany Foundation.

Individual Exhibitions

2002–2003 Institute of Contemporary Art, University of Pennsylvania, Philadelphia. Traveled: Arts Club of Chicago, Chicago, Illinois; Yerba Buena Center for the Arts, San Francisco, California; Seattle Art Museum, Seattle, Washington. Catalog.

1996 Richard Telles Gallery, Los Angeles, California. Jay Gorney Modern Art, New York City.

1994 Jack Hanley Gallery, San Francisco, California.

1993 Tom Cugliani Gallery, New York City.

1983 Broadway Espresso Gallery, Seattle, Washington.

Group Exhibitions

2001 "Alterations," James Graham & Sons, New York City.
"Postcards from the Edge," Sara Meltzer Gallery, New York City.

2000–2002 "Almost Warm and Fuzzy: Childhood and Contemporary Art," circulated by Independent Curators International. Traveled: Tacoma Art Museum, Tacoma, Washington; Scottsdale Museum of Contemporary Art, Scottsdale, Arizona; P.S.1 Contemporary Art Center/MOMA Affiliate, Long Island City, New York; Fundació "la Caixa," Barcelona, Spain; Crocker Art Museum, Sacramento, California; Art Gallery of Hamilton, Hamilton, Ontario, Canada; Cleveland Center for Contemporary Art, Cleveland, Ohio. Catalog.

2000 "Biennale de Lyon," Lyon, France.

1999–2000 "Bodies of Resistance," organized by Visual AIDS in conjunction with Real Artways, Hartford, Connecticut. Traveled: NSA Gallery, Durban, South Africa. Catalog.

1999 "Matter of Time," Dorsky Gallery, New York City. Brochure.
"Almost Warm and Fuzzy: Childhood and Contemporary Art," Des Moines Art Center, Des Moines, Iowa. Catalog.
"Summer Group Exhibition," Gorney Bravin + Lee, New York City.
"Collectors Collect Contemporary: 1990–1999," Institute of Contemporary Art, Boston, Massachusetts. Catalog.
"Recent Acquisitions," Whitney Museum of American Art, New York City.
"I'm Not Here: Constructing Identity at the Turn of the Century," Susquehanna Art Museum, Harrisburg, Pennsylvania. Catalog.

1998 "La Biennale de Montréal 98: 'Dreamcatchers,'" Centre International d'Art Contemporain, Montréal, Quebec, Canada.
American Academy of Arts and Letters, New York City.

1997 "The View from Denver," Museum Moderner Kunst, Vienna, Austria.
"La Biennale di Venezia: XL VII International Art Exhibition," Corderie Building, Venice, Italy. Catalog.
"As Time Goes By: History, Memory, and Sentimentality,"

Whitney Museum at Champion Plaza, Stamford, Connecticut.
"Art on the Edge of Fashion," Nelson Fine Arts Center, Arizona State University Art Museum, Tempe, Arizona. Catalog.
"Heart, Mind, Body, Soul: American Art in the 1990's," The Whitney Museum of American Art, New York City.
"Present Tense: Nine Artists in the Nineties," San Francisco Museum of Modern Art, San Francisco, California. Catalog.
"At the Threshold of the Visible: Minuscule and Small-Scale Art, 1964–1996," Herbert F. Johnson Museum of Art, Cornell University, Ithaca, New York. Traveled: Meyerhoff Galleries, Maryland Institute of Art, Baltimore, Maryland; Santa Monica Museum of Art, Santa Monica, California; Edmonton Art Gallery, Edmonton, Alberta, Canada.

1996 "Intermission," Basilico Fine Arts, New York City.
"Labor of Love," The New Museum of Contemporary Art, New York City.
"Biennale di Firenze: Art & Fashion, 1900–2000," Fort Belvedere, Florence, and Prato, Italy; Catalog.

1995 "Configura 2: Dialogue of Culture," City of Erfurt, Germany. Catalog.
"Fetishism: Power, Desire and Displacement," Traveled: Nottingham Castle Museum, Nottingham, England; Sainsbury Centre for the Visual Arts, University of East Anglia, Norwich, England. Catalog.
"Degrees of Abstraction: From Morris Louis to Mapplethorpe," Museum of Fine Arts, Boston, Massachusetts.
"Division of Labor: Women's Work," Bronx Museum of the Arts, Bronx, New York. Traveled: Museum of Contemporary Art, Los Angeles, California. Catalog.
"Woodworks," Michael Klein Gallery, New York City.

1994 "Toys/Art/Us," Castle Gallery, College of New Rochelle, New Rochelle, New York.
"Guys Who Sew," University Art Museum, University of California, Santa Barbara, California.
"Transformers: The Art of Multiphrenia," Center for Curatorial Studies, Bard College, Annandale-on Hudson, New York.
"Family Ties," P.P.O.W. Gallery, New York City.

"Lest We Forget/On Nostalgia," Takashimaya, New York City.
"Le Temps d'un Dessin," Galerie de l'Ecole des Beaux-Arts de Lorient, Lorient, France.

1993 "Anxious Art," Bernard Toale Gallery, Boston, Massachusetts.
"Mr. Sterling's Neighborhood," Christopher Grimes Gallery, Santa Monica, California.
"Fall from Fashion," Aldrich Museum of Contemporary Art, Ridgefield, Connecticut. Catalog.
"Charles LeDray/Siobhan Liddell," Jack Hanley Gallery, San Francisco, California.
"Le Principe de Realité," Villa Arson, Nice, France.
"Just what is it that makes today's home so different, so appealing?" Galerie Jennifer Flay, Paris, France.
"Bodyguard," Hohenhal und Bergen, Münich, Germany.

1992 "Vital Perfection: Sylvie Fleury, Gotscho, Charles LeDray," Galerie Urbi et Orbi, Paris, France.
"The Anti-Masculine," Kim Light Gallery, Los Angeles, California.
"Structural Damage: Charles LeDray, Joel Otterson, Gary Simmons, and Donald Moffett," Blum Helman Warehouse, New York City.

1991 "Sweet Dreams," Barbara Toll Gallery, New York City.
"Forbidden Games," Jack Tilton Gallery, New York City.
"*workworkworkworkwork*," Astor Place outdoor installation at Cooper Square, New York City.

Bibliography

Adams, Brooks and Lisa Liebmann, "Nothing Left Undone," Young Americans 2 (exhibition catalog). London: Saatchi Gallery, 1997.

Aletti, Vince. "Voice Choices." *The Village Voice* (28 January 1991).

"Art at the Millenium," *San Francisco Examiner* (11 September 1997).

"Art in Review: Charles LeDray." *The New York Times* (12 April 1996) C 28.

Ault, Julie, Gary Garrels, Bill Hayes, and John Weber. Present Tense: Nine Artists in the Nineties (exhibition catalog). San Francisco: San Francisco Museum of Modern Art, 1997.

Baker, Kenneth. "Nine Artists' Lessons of Recalling the Past in Present Tense." *San Francisco Chronicle* (Saturday, 13 September 1997).

Bonetti, David. *San Francisco Examiner* (24 May 1993).

Brunson, Jamie. Review. *Art Issues* (March–April 1994).

Cambon, Tricia. "S.F. M.o.M.A. Stays Simple in the Present Tense." *I. Journal* (15 September 1997).

Celant, Germano. *L'Espresso* (November 2000).

"Charles LeDray," *Sculpture* (Summer 1996).

Cohen, David. "Charles LeDray/Jay Gorney Modern Art." *Sculpture* (September 1996): 59–60.

Configura 2: (exhibition catalog), *Dialogue of Culture*. The City of Erfurt, Germany, 1995.

Cotter, Holland. "Art in Review: Charles LeDray." *The New York Times* (27 May 1994): E 36.

Cyphers, Peggy. Review. *Arts* (March 1991).

Fall from Fashion (exhibition catalog). Ridgefield, Connecticut: Aldrich Museum of Contemporary Art, 1993.

"Feminist Art, 1962 until Tomorrow Morning and International." *The New York Times* (17 March 1995).

Fetishism: Power, Desire and Displacement (exhibition catalog). The Brighton Museum and Art Gallery, Brighton, England; Nottingham Castle Museum, Nottingham, England; Sainsbury Centre for the Visual Arts, University of East Anglia, Norwich, England, 1995.

Fujimori, Manami. "Cute," *Bijutsu Techo*. [Tokyo] (February 1996): 14–15, 42–45.

"Galleries." *The New Yorker*. (24 June 1991).

Gilbert-Rolfe, Jeremy; Heather Sealy-Lineberry; and Marilyn A. Zeitlin. Art on the Edge of Fashion. (exhibition catalog), Tempe: Arizona State University Art Museum, 1997.

Glueck, Grace. "In Connecticut: Recent Nauman, Sentimental Memories and Black Culture." *The New York Times*. (18 July 1997): C 27.

Greene, David A. "Santa Barbara Fax." *Art Issues*. (January–February 1995).

Grundberg, Andy. "Present Tense: Nine Artists in the Nineties, SFMoMA." *Artforum* (February 1998): 87.

Hagen, Charles. "In Connecticut, Clothes, Photos and a Yale on Yale." *The New York Times* (July 1993): 23.

Harris, William. "Art and AIDS, Urgent Images." *Artnews* (May 1993): 120–123.

Helfand, Glan. "Just a moment. . . Nine Artists Quietly Endure Millennium Tension." *San Francisco Bay Examiner* (24 September 1997): 65–67.

Kandel, Susan. "Exquisite Miniatures of Sizable Seduction." *The Los Angeles Times* (22 June 1996): F 14.

Levin, Kim. "Voice Choices." *The Village Voice* (28 January 1992).

"Little Feats: Charles LeDray's Expansive Miniatures." *L.A. Weekly* (21–27 June 1996): 41.

Lord, M. G. "Women's Work Is (Sometimes) Done." *The New York Times* (19 February 1995).

Mahoney, Robert. "Charles LeDray." *Time Out New York* (24 April 1996): 29.

"'Matter of Time.'" *The New York Times* (September 1999): E 36.

Mellyn, Sean and Jonathan Van Dyke, eds. *I'm Not Here* (exhibition catalog). Harrisburgh: Susquehanna Art Museum, 1999.

Mileaf, Janine. "The House That Carrie Built: The Stettheimer Doll's House of the 1920's." guest edited by David A. Greene, *Art & Design: Art & the Home* [London], issue #51 (November–December 1996): 76–81, (reproduction).

Myers, Terry. Review. *Flash Art* (May 1991).

Newhall, Edith. "Art: Talent." *New York Magazine* (8 April 1996): 82.

Pedersen, Victoria. "Gallery Go Round," *Paper* (May 1996): 128.

Perchuk, Andrew. *Matter of Time: Jim Hodges, Charles LeDray, Michelle Segre and Jonathan Seliger* (exhibition catalog). New York: Dorsky Gallery, 1999.

Perl, Jed. "Group Dynamics." *Art & Antiques* (April 1991).

Raven, Arlene; Michelle Wallace; Lydia Yee. *Division of Labor: Women's Work* (exhibition catalog), Bronx Museum of the Arts, Bronx, 1995.

Retorno al País de las Maravillas, El arte contemporáneo y la infancia, (exhibition catalog), (Barcelona: Centre Cultural de la Fundació "la Caixa," 2001): 71.

Review. *San Francisco Examiner* (20 January 1994).

Rugoff, Ralph, and Susan Stewart. *At the Threshold of the Visible: Minuscule and Small-Scale Art, 1964–1996* (exhibition catalog), Independent Curators Inc., New York: 1997.

Saltz, Jerry. "It Don't Come Easy." *Arts Magazine* (April 1992): 23–24.

Review. *Art in America* (April 1993): 126–127.

Schjeldahl, Peter. "No Kidding." *The Village Voice* (23 April 1996): 91.

"Serious Side of an Infatuation with Fashion." *The New York Times*. (14 March 1997) C 28.

Seward, Keith. Review. *Artforum* (April 1993): 98.

"Sewing and Cooking." *The Village Voice* (9 February 1993).

Sischy, Ingrid. "Intertwined: Land of a Giant." *Interview* (April 1996): 60.

Smith, Roberta. "Charles LeDray." *The New York Times* (19 February 1993).

Smulders, Caroline, "Matière. . . risqué: artistes du corps, couturiers de l'image," *Art Press* (Paris): 35–40.

Taplin, Robert. "LeDray's Microcraft." *Art in America* (September 1996): 84–87.

Thea, Carolee. "Dispatch: 5th Lyon Biennale." *Sculpture* (December 2000): 82.

"The 10 Commandments of Taste," *Art & Auction*, November 1992.

Tully, Judd. "At the Edge. . . Seven Contemporary Collectors Talk." Interview with Robert J. Schiffler. *Art & Auction* (May 1997): 132.

Vanderlip, Dianne Perry. The View From Denver: Contemporary American Art from the Denver Art Museum (exhibition catalog). Museum Moderner Kunst Stiftung Ludwig Wein, Denver Art Museum, 1997.

"Voice Choices: Art Short List: Charles LeDray." *The Village Voice* (7 May 1996): 8.

"Voice Listings." *The Village Voice* (11 October 1995).

Wallach, Amei. "The Secrets of Childhood." *New York Newsday*. (13 January 1991).

Weinstein, Jeff, "Tender Buttons." *Artforum*. (Summer 1996): 96–99.

Yaeger, Lynn. "Art. . . la Mode." *The Village Voice*. (15 April 1997): 79.

Zimmer, Elizabeth. "It's Genius!: Artists Cheer the Best of the Year." contribution by LeDray, 24–26. *The Village Voice*. (7 January 1997): 26.

Zimmer, William. "Yes, there does exist a place for the sheerest of sentiment." *The New York Times* [Connecticut edition] (27 July 1997): section 13 CN, 14.

Zucker-Saltz, Lizzie. "Manufacturing Validity: The Ceramic Work of Art in the Age of Conceptual Production." *Art Papers* [Atlanta] (July–August, 1999): 28.

Artist's Acknowledgements

I would like to thank all those who generously funded this book and exhibition; all the lenders, especially SF MoMA, and the Whitney Museum of American Art; Claudia Gould and the staff of ICA; Russell Ferguson for his essay; Jack Woody and Twin Palms Publishers for the book design and printing; the directors and the staff of Sperone Westwater Gallery, New York, including GianEnzo Sperone, Angela Westwater, David Leiber, Karen Polack, Walter Biggs, Rachel Foullon, Michael Short; Kathy Cottong and the staff of the Arts Club of Chicago; Lisa Corrin, Tara Young, Michael McCafferty, Gail Joice, and the staff of the Seattle Art Museum; and Renny Pritikin and the staff of the Yerba Buena Center for the Arts, San Francisco. I also thank Jim Anderson and Bob Gindick, Ann Agee, Anonymous, Ralph Balass, Bobbie, Don, and Sean Barnhart, Mickey and Janice Cartin, Jenine Cirincione, Eileen and Michael Cohen, Scot, Julie and Hank Cohen, Tom Cugliani, Joel and Zoe Dictrow, John Defazio, Donald Fletcher, Kenneth L. Freed, Doug Gordon, Jay Gorney, John Groo, Jack Hanley, Rodney Hill, Susan and Michael Hort, Bill Jacobson, Max Lang, Sandie Ledray, Kim Lite, Ann Lovell, Rick Lyman, William Stone Mahoney, Frank Moore, Sam and Martha Peterson, Bob Roblee and Ron Johnson, Fred Rose, Jack Tilton, Barbara Toll, Matthew Wieland, Tom Woodruff, and Betty and George Woodman.

Colophon: This is the first edition of *Charles LeDray, Sculpture 1989-2002*. This book was printed and bound in Korea.

Book design is by Jack Woody and Arlyn Eve Nathan. The typeface selected is Diotima and Syntax. Diotima was designed by Gundrun Zapf-von Hesse in 1953 and Syntax was designed by Hans Eduard Meier in 1969.

COVER IMAGE:
Detail, *Come Together,*
1995–96, Fabric, thread,
embroidery floss, metal
34 ½ x 26 x 6 ½ inches
Collection San Francisco
Museum of Modern Art,
San Francisco
Purchased through a gift
of Kimberly S. L. Knight
and John B. Knight III

FRONT ENDPAPER:
Shelves, Studio Interiors
(works in progress) 2001
Photo: John Groo

BACK ENDPAPER:
Detail, Studio Interiors
(works in progress) 2001
Photo: John Groo

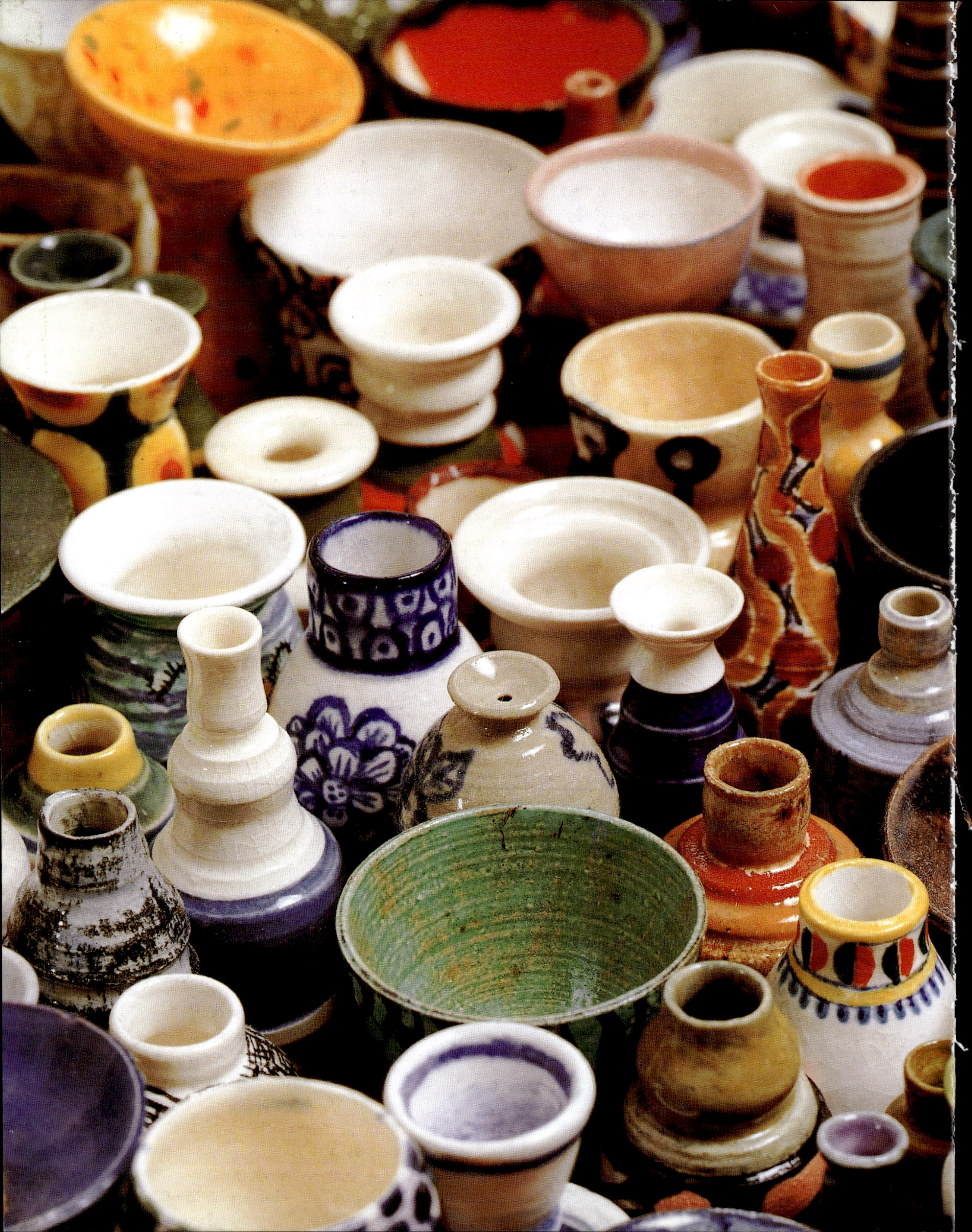